Prais

SECRETS *of* SWAGG

"While Randy Cohen wrote *Secrets of Swagger* as a guide for business owners and entrepreneurs, all I could think of as I read it was the treasure it would have been in my hands as a teenager with success aspirations. Randy personifies swagger and success—entrepreneurs should gift this book to kids with ambition. BAM!"

—**JACK DALY,** CEO at Professional Sales Coach

"This is a smart, fun, surprising book. With his typical savvy, humor, (and swagger), Randy connects lessons learned from JFK, George Clooney, Ronda Rousey, and many others. Not only a lively, unique how-to book for business, but also a terrific pep talk for everyday life. It left me fired up!"

—**CHRIS FOWLER,** ESPN Broadcaster

"You'll find no more powerful confidence boost!"

—**VERNE HARNISH,** Founder, Entrepreneurs' Organization (EO), Author of *Scaling Up: How a Few Make It . . . and Why the Rest Don't*

"Follow the advice in this book and you will walk with more swagger and confidence than John Wayne and Donald Trump combined!"

—**JEFFREY HAYZLETT,** Primetime TV & Podcast Host, Host of *C-Suite with Jeffrey Hayzlett*

"If you know Randy, you know he's quite a character. This book will give you more insight into his personality and philosophies!"

—TONY HSIEH, *New York Times* best-selling author of *Delivering Happiness* and CEO of Zappos.com

"The best thing about swagger is that it is contagious. Stepping into your own power inspires others to live their biggest life too—Randy's book gives plenty of pointers on how to do exactly that. If you have mountains to move, this book would be a good place to start."

—ROY SPENCE, Co-Founder and Chairman of GSD&M

Clark, 1/5/17

Great to meet you

Keep making a difference

SECRETS *of* SWAGGER

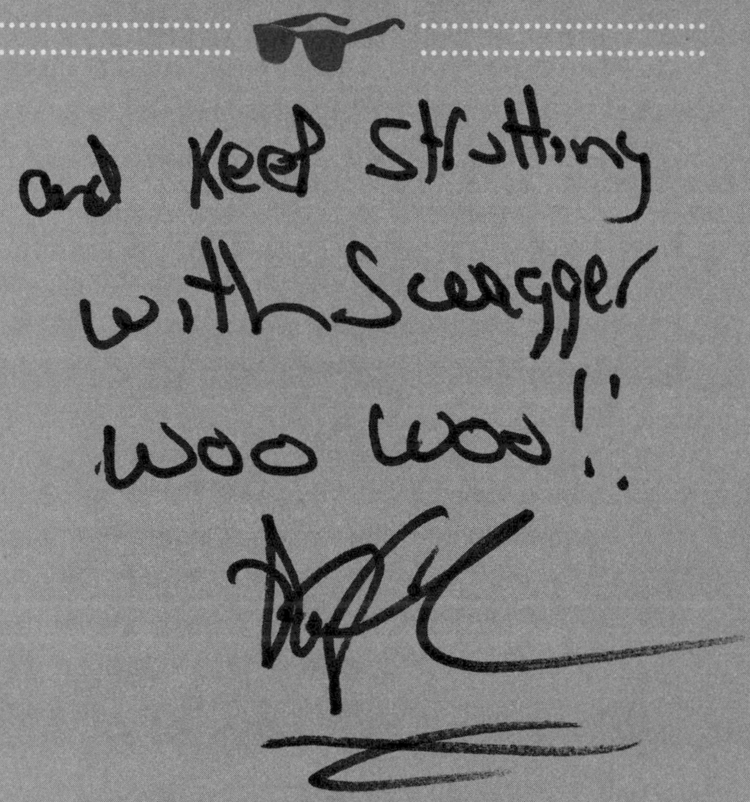

Dallas,

1/5/17

Great to meet you

Keep making a difference

Go Keep Strutting with 2 happy woo woo!

SECRETS *of* SWAGGER

HOW TO OWN YOUR COOL IN LIFE AND BUSINESS

RANDY COHEN

GREENLEAF
BOOK GROUP PRESS

Published by Greenleaf Book Group Press
Austin, Texas
www.gbgpress.com

Distributed by Greenleaf Book Group

For ordering information or special discounts for bulk purchases, please contact Greenleaf Book Group at PO Box 91869, Austin, TX 78709, 512.891.6100.

Design and composition by Greenleaf Book Group
Cover design by Greenleaf Book Group

Cataloging-in-Publication data is available.

Print ISBN: 978-1-62634-377-1

eBook ISBN: 978-1-62634-378-8

Part of the Tree Neutral® program, which offsets the number of trees consumed in the production and printing of this book by taking proactive steps, such as planting trees in direct proportion to the number of trees used: www.treeneutral.com

Printed in the United States of America on acid-free paper

16 17 18 19 20 10 9 8 7 6 5 4 3 2 1

First Edition

CONTENTS

PREFACE

Chutzpah. Charisma. The cool factor . . . Call it what you want, but it's all about that swagger! Confidence will take you far in business and in life, but you've got to have it before you can use it. And the more you have, the further it will take you . . .

Of course, not everyone has the kind of self-assurance and swagger that lets you be that one head rising above a sea of sameness, but the more you develop your personal charisma, the greater your chances of success. There's no denying it: People with confidence are cool, and cool people have all the fun!

Confidence is sexy. Confidence is powerful. But confidence is also a choice! You can be a wallflower or you can be a beautiful bouquet in full bloom. Whether you're an introvert, an extrovert, or an ambivert (somewhere in the middle), confidence and swagger can be learned, and can transform your life from ordinary to truly extraordinary. Doesn't matter if you're a guy or a gal, big or small, scientist, secretary, or sales manager. When you're confident, you're more powerful. And swagger is just confidence with an attitude.

So let's talk swagger. The word alone conjures up all kinds of images. Who do you think of when you hear the word "swagger"? Frank Sinatra? John Wayne? MMA fighter Ronda Rousey? Or maybe Mick Jagger or Kanye West? Swagger can sometimes have a negative connotation when someone acts like an arrogant jerk. (Are you listening, Kanye?) But, either way, you can't deny that swagger brings confidence!

For my entire twenty-five-year career as the CEO (Chief Energizing Officer) at TicketCity, I've seen swagger in all its forms: the good, the bad, and the ugly. My unique position (and really cool job) has given me access to some of the biggest names in sports, music, movies, and business. I've been courtside, ringside, and inside at some of the greatest events on the planet—from Olympics and Super Bowls to Final Fours, Kentucky Derbies, and sold-out mega-concerts.

From backstage to boardrooms, this unique perspective has given me an inside look at the "science" of swagger, and how some people reach amazing heights of success just by channeling their inner power and "strutting their stuff" all the way to the bank.

Swagger is about self-confidence and creating your own unique personal brand that can carry you through life. It's not about arrogance; it's about believing in yourself and having the courage to be fully self-expressed. Swagger is not about rich or poor, male or female, black or white. It's about maintaining a positive attitude and carrying yourself with pride and dignity. Swagger is about being the best possible version of you, and owning it.

In the pages that follow, I'll be sharing my experience and my take on "swagger." On living large because you're living well. On owning your personal power and using it to make the world a little brighter. This book is designed to help you develop your own individual brand of swagger.

We'll be looking at people who personify swagger—both dead and alive, famous and lesser known, good and bad, along with a few "swaggerlicious" people I know personally. All the stories and case studies will give ideas, inspiration, and insight to help you find your own inner power so you can swagger your way to greater success.

Enjoy the journey with me!

—Randy Cohen, 2016

1

COLLABORATION

"Alone we can do so little;
together we can do so much."
—Helen Keller

You may find it odd to start a book about swagger with the topic of collaboration, but the simple truth is that no one succeeds on their own, and success is hard to come by unless you're standing on the shoulders of others. While "swagger" may be thought of as an individual trait, collaboration may well be the secret sauce of success.

The problem is that it's easy to talk about collaboration and teamwork. In fact, the entire concept of teamwork has almost become a cliché. The trouble with teamwork is that it's often included in mission statements and pep talks, but it's rarely executed in the real world. Unless you weave it into your company's DNA, collaboration is nothing more than lip service.

Fortunately, true teamwork doesn't have to be an empty promise or a lofty, unachievable goal. We've worked very diligently over the years to make collaboration part of the fabric of our company. We really do think of our team as a family, and we go to great lengths to build a strong sense of community here at TicketCity. We're consistently named one of the "Best Places to Work" in Austin, Texas, and we take great pride in our team and our community service.

Our company continues to thrive at twenty-five years young because we operate on the guiding principles of passion, fun, relationships, integrity, respect, and innovation. We have these principles mounted on huge posters throughout the office, so we can be reminded of them every day.

Obviously, it takes more than posters to instill a company culture of collaboration, so we practice what we preach. I make it a point to take my team members to lunch annually, and I also make sure to get out from behind my desk and walk around the office. I call it the three o'clock stroll, and it gives me a chance to see what everyone is working on and stay connected.

Sir Richard Branson, whom I recently had the pleasure of spending time with, and whom we profile in this book, is a big proponent of MBWA, or Management by Walking Around. It has to be more than just handshakes and high-fives—you've got to really listen and ask questions. It's just another way to show your employees that you care about the work they're doing.

We also build collaboration and teamwork with company parties, retreats, and even spur-of-the-moment celebrations. During the NBA play-offs, for example, we brought in one of those basketball dunk hoops and got everyone involved in a spontaneous competition. On other occasions, we'll have catered meals or bring in a margarita machine on a Friday afternoon.

The first Tuesday of every month we also do an "office all-around." We bring the entire team together to give one another "shout-outs" and recognize and acknowledge all the great work that's being done. It gives everyone a chance to boost one another up and offer positive feedback.

In addition to retreats and company events, we also do "charity weeks" and give our team members an opportunity to work together in the community to help out local organizations. We'll work with the food bank or the local animal shelter, to support local nonprofits, but we're also creating great bonding experiences for our employees.

Speaking of opportunities for building camaraderie, a few years back we took the entire fifty-person staff on a vacation/retreat to Cancun in Mexico. It was our chance to celebrate success together and reward the team for all their hard work.

Many of our employees and managers have been with the company for most of our twenty-five years. In fact, most of the management team has been here for an average of eighteen years! That's something that has become a rarity in most organizations. Why do we enjoy such loyalty and teamwork at TicketCity? The short answer is that we work at it—and not just at annual meetings or company retreats, but every single day.

So even though our company benefits are top notch, we do our best to go above and beyond finding the "little things" that make a big difference. I have lunch with everyone on our staff at least once a year, and I often take employees to lunch on their birthdays. We make a big deal of employee milestones like anniversaries and deeds well done. It's that personal touch that goes beyond any words in your mission statement. It's what you do every day to show you care.

In a recent white paper from MetLife entitled "Culture Happens: How to Ensure It's What You Want," former Southwest Airlines and JetBlue Chief People Officer Ann Rhoades says, "When you have a great culture, people want to come to work." She also points out that company culture comes down to establishing a set of expected values and behaviors: "It can encompass how a company treats its employees and how employees treat customers."

"The best cultures are by design," says Rhoades. In other words, if "fun" is one of your company values—like it is here at TicketCity—then "define what that means, whether it's being lighthearted with customers or using work time for celebrations and company parties."

Once you've established your company's core values, maintaining that company culture is an ongoing process. Great company cultures and values go hand in hand and it's very important to instill those values throughout your workforce.

You can also make sure that some of the core values are part of the compensation and benefits package. Since we're in the events business, one of our unique perks is allowing our team to experience some of the coolest events on the planet, including the Super Bowl, the Final Four, the Kentucky Derby, and the Masters.

We also sponsor the TicketCity Cactus Bowl, and encourage the team to do the honors of performing the coin toss at the stadium, or delivering the trophy to the winning team at the end of the game. Giving your team the chance to experience these once-in-a-lifetime opportunities increases loyalty, employee retention, and a sense of community.

However, the real test of teamwork and collaboration is in the tough times. It's important to share the credit but also take the blame. As the CEO, you can't ever throw anyone under the bus. You've got to be willing to take that hit for your team.

During Super Bowl XLIX in Arizona, we had a ticket debacle where some of our suppliers didn't come through with tickets that were sold to our customers. It was just a terrible situation all around, with people who were expecting tickets not receiving them. Can you imagine thinking you're going to the Super Bowl, only to find out your tickets never materialized? It would have been easy to assign blame and point fingers, but we really met the situation head-on and were very proactive about it. There was really no use sugarcoating it—we simply had to bite the bullet and take the hit. It was our ultimate responsibility.

However, I was extremely proud of the way our entire team conducted themselves during this difficult situation, and I wanted to make sure they realized their efforts did not go unnoticed. I also wanted to make sure we singled out a few team members, acknowledging that they were difference makers. So, a few days after the event, I sent out the following note:

> Hello, everyone, now that the dust is starting to settle, I wanted to reach out and say thank you for going above and beyond during this unprecedented event that impacted the ticket industry as a whole. I could not be more proud of our team, who stepped up in a tough situation and met it head-on.
>
> Bryan and his customer service team were extraordinary. I personally watched Matt and Bryan do anything and everything to take care of our clients as best they could. Ted and the service team in Austin did an amazing job listening, comforting, and keeping our clients informed.
>
> Alex set up a restaurant viewing party, and customers were super-grateful. Clark and the accounting department worked logistics and answered questions on accounting needs. Zach, AB, and Ashley were terrific in clarifying social media concerns.
>
> Caroline, Lindsay, and Ryan M. were fantastic in keeping things organized in Phoenix, and Lou and Rick worked hard trying to obtain tickets for clients' unfilled orders. There are many names I didn't mention, but you know who you are and thanks for stepping up.
>
> I've been around this industry for a long time, and it's not what we say or do that makes a difference for all our customers, it's how we show up and make them feel.

> We did not please one hundred percent of our clients, but we can be extremely proud of how we did our best to handle a difficult situation. I've been telling everyone that this was "the best worst experience of my life," and there is no one else I would rather have shared this journey with than everyone here. Thank you, thank you, thank you for all your support, caring, and heart.

Collaboration doesn't just happen, and it can't be guaranteed by a fancy mission statement. Teamwork needs to be weaved throughout the entire thread of your company and with that in mind, here are seven suggestions for creating a collaborative work environment:

How to build collaboration in your organization

1. **Be all inclusive.** No one likes being left out! So, the first step in creating a positive, collaborative environment is being inclusive. Think about what Gravity Payments CEO Dan Price did a while back. He took a $930,000 pay cut so he could raise the minimum salary at his 120-person payment-processing company to $70,000. At a company where the average pay was $48,000 per year, the raise affected seventy workers, thirty of whom saw their salaries double. That's how you build loyalty!
2. **Prove that you care.** Tackling salary inequities is certainly one way to prove that you care about your employees, but even smaller gestures can have an impact. Something as simple as taking team members to lunch and

celebrating their milestones sends a positive signal to workers that you care about them personally.

3. **Celebrate victories together.** From our monthly "office all-arounds" and shout-outs to annual retreats, we make it a point to celebrate together and share victories big and small. Don't let those opportunities to share success get lost in the day-to-day activities.

4. **Share the credit/Take the blame.** Another way to celebrate and build a sense of community is to always share the credit, and be ready and willing to take the blame. Sometimes the boss has to "take a bullet" for the team—the buck stops with you!

5. **Never ask your staff to do anything you wouldn't do yourself.** Leaders must lead by example, and that means being willing to get into the trenches and get your hands dirty with the rest of the team. You'll earn the respect of your staff, and they'll be willing to work harder for you when they see you in the trenches with them.

6. **Make morale building more than just lip service.** All of the tips above can go a long way to building and maintaining employee morale, but it really has to be part of your company's everyday culture—not a once-a-year event. And, again, there are a lot of intangibles, like simply showing appreciation and thanking team members for a job well done.

7. **Develop a sense of community.** Creating a team that feels like a family is a difficult balancing act. Here at

> TicketCity, we realize that family members sometimes have differences and, like family, we're not afraid to challenge one another or engage in healthy debates. It's not all wine and roses all the time. Sometimes things get heated, but like any family we work out the differences, find common ground, and ultimately do what's best for the family/company.

Collaboration goes beyond just team building with your employees. The most successful businesses build collaboration and cooperation with vendors, associates, colleagues and, of course, customers! We cherish the great relationships we have with our clients, and we also work hard to make sure we're being great citizens in our community.

So, beyond the chemistry that we have among the staff, we're fortunate to forge those long-lasting relationships in the community as well. We established the TicketCity Annual Scholarship Program to give students an opportunity to earn $3,000 toward their college expenses. Being in the ticket business, where so many of our activities revolve around college sports, it was natural for us to support not just the student-athletes, but also the student-fans!

As we say on our website:

> TicketCity loves college sports. From the first tailgate party of football season to the final round of March Madness, we can't get enough of it. Focus is almost always on the student-athletes, but we know it wouldn't be the same

> without the support of the student-fans. Every school has its own unique traditions, and we want to hear why those traditions are so special to you.
>
> This is why we created the TicketCity Annual College Scholarship Program. We want to thank the students for turning an ordinary game into a tradition-rich, high-energy event that will be remembered forever. All students have to do is write an essay about something they already love, the college sports experience, and they can earn $3,000 to help pay for school.

When you think of collaboration, think beyond the traditional definition of "teamwork," and consider the many ways you can build collaboration and relationships among your colleagues and peers. Developing a wide network of business associates gives you access to a much bigger "brain trust" of ideas and expertise.

From the early days of my career, I made it a point to get involved with peer groups and associations like the Young Entrepreneurs' Organization (now known simply as the Entrepreneurs' Organization) and other civic groups to expand my circle and learn from others. I've continued networking and being involved with other "mastermind" groups, and it's been a big factor in my company's success.

For many years, I've been involved with the Entrepreneurial Masters Program. Here's a brief description of what this amazing group is all about:

The Entrepreneurial Masters Program (EMP) brings together 65 remarkable entrepreneurs—each a founder or co-founder of a company that grosses more than US$1 million—for four days at the MIT Endicott House, located in Dedham, Massachusetts.

- To identify and bring together the next generation of entrepreneurial giants—the next Bill Gates or Richard Branson.
- To provide the kind of intense blending of practice and theory that is necessary to excel in this era and to do so in a format that fits your busy schedule.
- To offer this high-quality program at a price that is less than half the cost of comparable programs (all of our efforts go into quality programming and facilities, not fancy promotions).

The focus is on leadership. The sessions are rigorous. In short, we bring you the best, at a time when you need it, in a way that fits both your schedule and budget.

The value of spending time with other high-level peers and colleagues cannot be understated. The relationships you build at events like these can truly make or break your business.

Groups like Birthing of Giants give you a subjective "board of directors" where you can find ideas, information, and support. Of course, you also develop friendships and partnerships that can last a lifetime.

Obviously, there are tremendous benefits to being part of a group like the Entrepreneurs' Organization, because it gives you access to an influential network of more than 11,000 business owners spread across forty-eight countries.

However, you may want to create a mastermind group that's closer to home, where you can meet face-to-face more often. Some local colleagues and I started a small group called the Austin Council of Entrepreneurs (ACEs), and we meet in person every month to brainstorm and support one another. This particular group is made up of about a dozen Austin entrepreneurs, and we've been meeting regularly for the past five years. It's invaluable to have associates outside your own internal management team so you can get different perspectives.

Actress and *SNL* alum Amy Poehler may have hit the nail on the head with her take on collaboration: "You can't do it alone. As you navigate through the rest of your life, be open to collaboration. Other people and other people's ideas are often better than your own. Find a group of people who challenge and inspire you. Spend a lot of time with them, and it will change your life. No one is here today because they did it on their own."

If you're looking for networking groups to join, I have participated in several that have helped influence my growth personally and professionally.

- Entrepreneurs' Organization—founded in 1987 by Verne Harnish, who is one of the greatest global thought leaders on entrepreneurship I have ever met. It was originally called YEO (Young Entrepreneurs' Organization and had an age-out limit of forty). It later became EO (The Entrepreneurs' Organization) and specializes in monthly forum groups for entrepreneurs and connecting over 10,000 peers. Entrepreneurs must have over $1 million in revenues from their company to be eligible for membership. EO provides access to mentors, coaches, and global educational networking events. EO also has a group healthcare option through the Healthcare Foundation.

- Vistage—Founded in 1957, Vistage has been helping CEOs improve their companies and grow their businesses by exchanging ideas and passing along advice through forum groups. These groups have a paid moderator who also does the recruiting of business owners. It's like a high-end business fraternity that costs around $15,000 a year for membership. Today, Vistage has more than 18,000 members and holds well over 16,000 meetings per year. If you want to network, speak with mentors, or attend yearly economic events with world renowned speakers, Vistage is the way to go for any serious entrepreneur.

- Young Presidents' Organization—Ray Hickok founded YPO in 1950. Today, the organization has approximately

22,000 business-leader members in more than 125 countries. YPO is a high-end extension of EO requiring members to have at least $25 million in revenue or 50 employees. It specializes in business forum groups and creates opportunities to bounce ideas off or seek advice from a global network. The YPO also collects performance metrics and trends for quarterly reports, networking events, and roundtable discussions. The YPO not only assists you with your business life, but also with your personal life by providing guidance for family members and couples' retreats. This is a great organization if you're under forty-five.

- BBB—The Better Business Bureau in your city is a tremendous organization to join where you can network, learn, and grow. They often have monthly and annual events and are extremely cost-effective to join. BBBs set standards for ethical business behavior and monitor compliance. They lead the way in advancing marketplace trust by encouraging and supporting best practices through engaging with and educating consumers and businesses.

- Chamber of Commerce—Your local chamber helps build a strong community by connecting its members to people, business, and issues important to business success. Chambers provide unique opportunities for business leaders to influence civic, social, and business initiatives that support community growth. It creates a climate of growth and success that benefits all business.

- The Entrepreneurs Club—TEC may not technically be a membership organization, but attending any of the ten or so events or seminars a year gives you the chance to network, exchange ideas with peers, or sit in on discussions surrounding the latest market trends. Events also include influential speakers.

- Gazelles Inc.—Gazelles is all about helping your business scale up. They provide executive education, coaching, strategy, and technology services to help mid-market companies around the world build and execute a strategic plan. Gazelles provides executive education through live events and online seminars. They feature some of the leading business experts, including Seth Godin, Pat Lencioni, Geoff Smart, and Jack Stack. They also sponsor best-practices trips to Dell, GE, Microsoft, and Southwest Airlines. Founded by Verne Harnish in 1997, they send out weekly invites that are extremely helpful in best-practice learning for your business.

Swagger Success Story:
In each chapter, we're including charisma case studies for a look at those who've found success with swagger. Use these real-life stories to find ways to bring more success into your business and life . . .

SWAGGER SUCCESS STORY
LADY GAGA

No one does swagger quite like Lady Gaga. The thirty-year-old pop star burst onto the scene seemingly out of nowhere, taking the music industry by storm. Of course, "overnight success" rarely happens overnight, and Lady Gaga's ascent to fame was actually a long and circuitous path.

Gaga was born Stefani Joanne Angelina Germanotta in Manhattan in March 1986. While she enjoyed an affluent upbringing on New York City's Upper West Side, she describes her parents as working class—setting a good example for the value of hard work. She attended a private all-girl Catholic school and was described as studious and disciplined. However, Gaga later admitted that she felt out of place in high school and was often teased for being too provocative and too eccentric.

She began playing the piano at age four, was writing songs at thirteen, and was performing at open-mic nights by the time she was fourteen. She played the lead in her high school's theatrical productions and musicals, and even scored a small role as an extra in a *Sopranos* episode in 2001.

After high school, she applied and was accepted to Collaborative Arts Project 21 (CAP21), part of NYU's prestigious Tisch School of the Arts. She was one of only twenty students to gain early admission at the age of seventeen. However, she dropped out of the CAP21 program in her sophomore year to focus solely on her music career.

In addition to writing and recording a few of her own songs, Gaga formed a band with a couple of her NYU classmates, and the Stefani Germanotta Band (SGBand) became a fixture of New York's Lower East Side club scene.

Gaga met record producer Rob Fusari in 2006, and the two began dating. Fusari compared some of her harmonies to Freddie Mercury of Queen, and would often sing Queen's "Radio Ga Ga" when she entered the recording studio. One day Fusari texted her as "Radio Ga Ga," but the auto-correct changed the text to "Lady Gaga." Fusari claims she texted back and said, "That's it! Don't ever call me Stefani again." The rest, as they say, is history!

She was signed to Def Jam Recordings in 2006, after their head of A&R noticed her "unusual and provocative" performance, but she was dropped by the label after only three months. This became a dark period for Gaga, and she became increasingly experimental and avant-garde. At one point, she even became a go-go dancer at a dive bar on the Lower East Side. "It represented freedom to me," Gaga would later say about the experience. "I went to a Catholic school, but it was on the New York underground that I found myself."

During this experimental period, Gaga met performance artist "Lady Starlight," who is credited with helping mold Lady Gaga's onstage persona. The pair began performing together and were even invited to the Lollapalooza music festival in 2007.

Gaga seemed to find her musical niche once her electronic dance music evolved, and she began adding pop melodies and aspects of "glam rock" influenced by David Bowie and Queen. She signed a music publishing deal with Sony, and she began to write songs for Britney Spears, New Kids on the Block, Fergie, and The Pussycat Dolls.

Singer-songwriter Akon noticed her vocal abilities and convinced Interscope Geffen A&M Chairman and CEO Jimmy Iovine to sign her. Despite her new record deal, Gaga admitted that there were fears about her being too racy, dance oriented, and underground for the mainstream music market. To that, she defiantly replied: "My name is Lady Gaga, I've been on the music scene for years, and I'm telling you, this is what's next."

In 2008, Gaga moved to Los Angeles to work on her debut album, called *The Fame*. While the record was slow to get airplay, the songs "Just Dance" and "Poker Face" became sleeper hits, and the album was eventually nominated for Record of the Year at the 2009 Grammy Awards. *The Fame* would go on to stay on the charts for 106 weeks and sell over 12 million copies worldwide.

As Gaga's follow-up albums and tours brought her even greater success, she also expanded into groundbreaking business endeavors and partnerships. The 52nd Annual Grammy Awards opened with a piano duet with Elton John, and she was asked to open for Michael Jackson and his "This Is It" tour before his death in June 2009. Her 2011 performances at Madison Square Garden in New York City became an Emmy Award–winning HBO special.

Gaga also collaborated with consumer products companies as her empire and influence expanded. In 2009, she partnered with Monster Cable Products to create a pair of in-ear jewel-encrusted headphones called Heartbeats. "They are designed to be the first ever fashion accessories that double as the absolute best sonically sounding headphones in the world," said the singer-turned-entrepreneur.

Gaga also partnered with Polaroid in 2010 as their creative director. In an effort to combine the iconic history of Polaroid and instant film with the digital era, Gaga unveiled a trio of new products called Grey

Label, which included a pair of picture-taking sunglasses, a paperback-sized mobile printing unit, and a new and improved version of the traditional Polaroid camera that made its debut at the 2011 Consumer Electronics Show.

In 2012, she announced her first fragrance in association with Coty, called Lady Gaga Fame, and in 2014 she would become the face and centerpiece for Versace's "Lady Gaga for Versace" campaign.

Gaga also collaborated musically with Tony Bennett on an album called *Cheek to Cheek*. The collection of jazz standards became Gaga's third consecutive number-one record in the United States, and it won a Grammy Award for Best Traditional Pop Vocal Album. The duo recorded a concert special for PBS, called *Tony Bennett and Lady Gaga: Cheek to Cheek Live!*, and the pair also embarked on the Cheek to Cheek Tour, which played a total of thirty-six shows across Europe and North America during the first half of 2015.

Gaga surprised everyone with a remarkable performance during the 2015 Academy Awards when she sang a tribute to *The Sound of Music*. Her performance was the most talked-about moment on the Oscars and on social media, triggering over 214,000 interactions per minute globally on Facebook.

Much of Gaga's swagger comes from her own confidence and the empowering messages she shares with fans. The music and fashion icon seems comfortable in her own, often outrageous skin, and she's never been afraid to soak up the spotlight. "Fame for me is not external, it's internal," says Gaga. "So I've been famous for a long time."

Gaga is noted for her diverse contributions to the music industry via her self-empowering messages, unique fashion, and lavish live performances. She has sold over 28 million albums and has singles sales of 140 million, making her one of the best-selling musicians of all time. Her worldwide concert tours have already grossed more than $300 million in revenue, and she's estimated to have a net worth of over $100 million. She achieved all of this before she turned thirty years old!

Other achievements for Gaga include six Grammy Awards, thirteen MTV Video Music Awards, and thirteen Guinness World Records, and she is the first artist to ever receive a Songwriters Hall of Fame's Contemporary Icon Award. She consistently appears on *Billboard* magazine's Artists of the Year lists and *Forbes*'s power and earnings rankings. In 2013, *Time* magazine listed Gaga as one of the Most Influential People of the Decade.

Outside her music, she is lauded for her many philanthropic endeavors and social activism, including LGBT rights and HIV/AIDS prevention. In 2012, Lady Gaga established the Born This Way Foundation (BTWF), a nonprofit organization that focuses on youth empowerment as well as issues such as self-confidence, well-being, anti-bullying, mentoring, and career development. She's also been extremely active and generous in her contributions to relief efforts for natural disasters like the 2010 Haiti earthquake, the 2011 tsunami in Japan, and Hurricane Sandy in 2012.

SEVEN BUSINESS LESSONS FROM LADY GAGA

Gaga may be a singer-songwriter, fashion icon, and activist, but she can also teach you a thing or two about running a business. Here are seven lessons from the pop star's playbook that we can adapt for our companies:

1. **Build a Community**—Everyone talks about finding your "tribe," or creating a community, but Gaga has actually done it magnificently. She refers to her rabid fan base as

"little monsters," and calls herself "Mother Monster." She has even created a social network specifically for her fans at www.littlemonsters.com. What can you do to rally your customers around your cause?

2. **Constantly Evolve**—With Gaga's outlandish fashion and many diverse endeavors, it seems as though she is constantly reinventing herself. In today's short-attention-span society, you've got to keep your customers interested and engaged in new and different ways. Think about the things your company could do to stay relevant with your audience.

3. **Be Everywhere**—With social media and a twenty-four-hour news cycle, maintaining your visibility may not be as difficult as you might imagine. You don't necessarily have to go "full throttle" for years at a time like Lady Gaga, but staying visible through social media and online video can give you a presence even when you're offline.

4. **Form Unlikely Alliances**—Lady Gaga and Tony Bennett may seem like an unlikely pairing, but it produced a very lucrative partnership. (It's a bit like mixing chocolate and peanut butter and coming up with the Reese's Peanut Butter Cup!) There may be unique alliances that you can form to breathe new life into your venture.

5. **Leverage Social Media**—Gaga has nearly 55 million Twitter followers and another 9 million on Instagram. Her YouTube videos are the most-viewed videos in history, where she holds the record with over a billion video views! Fortunately, you don't need those kinds of numbers to have an impact on social

media. Make sure your social platforms are active and keep your customers in the loop.

6. **Embrace Your Brand**—Lady Gaga thrives on being provocative, and she celebrates what makes her different. Obviously, it takes some chutzpah to wear a dress made out of raw meat to an awards show, but Gaga gets her point across and truly embraces her uniqueness. What can your company do to celebrate what makes you distinctive? Don't fall prey to distractions. Stay true to who you are.

7. **Give Back**—Gaga sets an excellent example with her many philanthropic and charity endeavors. Her Born This Way Foundation works on youth empowerment and anti-bullying initiatives, and she is a strong proponent of gay rights. Consider the various ways you and your company can give back to the community where you live and work.

2

CHARISMA: SWAGGER YOUR WAY TO SUCCESS

"You only go around once, but if you play your cards right, once is enough."

—Frank Sinatra

One of William Shakespeare's most-often-cited quotes (from *As You Like It*) is "All the world's a stage, and all the men and women merely players." (Heck, rock band Rush even used the line in their hit song "Limelight.")

If you want to succeed on the stage of life and truly be a "player," then you've got to have some measure of swagger.

You don't necessarily have to be a "10" on the "Swagger Scale" like Frank Sinatra or John F. Kennedy, and you certainly don't need to be "over the top" like Lady Gaga, but you've got to believe in yourself and be comfortable in your own skin. Jeweler to the stars Harry Winston once said: "People will stare. Make it worth their while." You gotta love that attitude.

No one is born with charisma—it's learned over the course of time and through experiences. But whether or not you grew up with self-confidence, it's something you have to develop for success as an adult. Let's face it: You don't see a lot of movie stars, world leaders, rock stars, or successful CEOs who are skittish, timid, or insecure. A certain amount of swagger can be a very good thing.

But how do you develop swagger if you're not naturally gregarious or self-confident? That's the million-dollar question, and it's what we'll be addressing throughout this book. You've got to start with building your confidence, because that's the key ingredient for having any kind of charisma or personal appeal.

In order to cultivate confidence, you've got to be happy. Don't worry, that doesn't mean you need to walk around with a fake smile pasted on your face or be Mr. or Mrs. Sunshine 24/7. Nobody is always happy—it's more a matter of having a generally upbeat outlook on life and seeing the glass as half-full. Or finding the good in every situation and being a kind-hearted person with a positive self-image. Miserable people aren't known for having swagger, and no one wants to be around miserable people.

Self-confidence, a positive outlook, and a certain style of grace under pressure are the cornerstones of charisma, and they are characteristics that can be cultivated when you make a conscious effort and an unwavering commitment to develop the requisite skills.

With that in mind, let's dive right in with ten practical tips for developing more personal charisma and upping your "swagger factor":

1. **Believe in yourself**—Nothing is more swaggerlicious than self-confidence. You've got to project poise, passion, and purpose to "own" the room. "Owning it" can also come in the form of a quiet confidence. You don't have to be loud or boisterous to be self-assured. Just be secure about who you are and others will feel that vibe.
2. **Different is better**—Embrace your differences and celebrate what makes you unique. Gaga's outfits are over the top. Bill Clinton played the saxophone on late-night TV. Frank Sinatra hung out with mobsters and wasn't afraid to get in a scuffle. Elvis sang and moved unlike any singer that came before him. Being different is not only good, being different makes you memorable, and as the saying goes, "Be a voice, not an echo!"
3. **Show some enthusiasm**—There's no chance of success without energy and enthusiasm, and there's certainly no swagger without enthusiasm. You've got to have that "fire within," and if you don't have it, then you'd better

fake it 'til you make it. The great thing about enthusiasm is that if you simply act enthusiastic, you'll be enthusiastic! Ralph Waldo Emerson said: "Enthusiasm is the mother of effort, and without it nothing great was ever achieved." But perhaps an even better quote on the subject came from the great Vince Lombardi, who said, "If you aren't fired with enthusiasm, you will be fired with enthusiasm!"

4. **Dress the part**—Of course you've heard the old adage "Dress for success," but a more appropriate strategy for developing personal charisma may be to look the part. Dress for the job you want, not the job you have. How you look and how you carry yourself are essential ingredients for building your reputation and getting your swagger on. Just ask Lady Gaga!

5. **Take a stand**—If you want to be regarded as a person of principle, then you've got to be willing to take a stand, and then remain firm and steadfast in your beliefs. But be sure to make the distinction between stubbornness and conviction. Speak up. Have an opinion. Be original, unique, and authentic.

6. **Listen more than you talk**—God gave you two ears and one mouth, so it's just common sense that you should listen twice as much as you speak! If you don't buy that logic, then consider that being a good listener is one of the most vital qualities for success in any endeavor. As TED speaker and author Simon Sinek notes, "There

is a difference between listening and waiting for your turn to speak." Listening is a lost art waiting for you to reclaim it.

7. **Exude confidence, but not arrogance**—Stand proud, walk tall, strut your stuff! But as you walk, proud as a peacock, be sure never to cross that fine line from confidence over to arrogance. Because confidence is cool, but being arrogant or condescending is not cool! Most people would agree that George Clooney is confident, but Kayne West is often considered arrogant. Understand the subtle difference and you're on the right track.

8. **Be decisive, never waffle**—"Ummm, I'm not sure . . . maybe . . . " These are not the words of those with swagger. People with confidence and charisma are not afraid to make decisions and stick with their commitments. It's not about always being right; it's about not being afraid to be wrong. Winners take risks and make the tough calls, without being weak or wishy-washy. No one respects the "waffler."

9. **Genuinely care about others**—Author Robert Brault says, "Charisma is not so much getting people to like you as getting people to like themselves when you're around." There's often a misconception that people with swagger are self-centered when, in fact, the opposite is true. Being self-assured is not the same thing as being self-absorbed. Real swagger comes when you show concern for others and you make them feel good.

As Maya Angelou once said: "At the end of the day people won't remember what you said or did, they will remember how you made them feel."

10. **Step up**—Living large, making a difference, and leading with confidence will require you to step it up. Whether you're a CEO or a CPA, there will be occasions when you're called upon to lead. You may be shy or you may be reluctant, but you'll have to step up, take control, and lead the way. In my company, as the boss, I understand the importance of sharing the credit and taking the blame. President Dwight D. Eisenhower put it eloquently when he said, "Leadership consists of nothing but taking responsibility for everything that goes wrong and giving your subordinates credit for everything that goes well." That's how you step up. The good news about building your swagger factor is that you can be more confident, more self-assured, and more charismatic if you simply choose to be. It's really just a matter of stepping into your personal power and becoming fully self-expressed. Even if you're not naturally outgoing, you can develop a quiet confidence and "coolness" that radiates strength. After all, a real lion doesn't have to roar! As motivation speaker Les Brown points out: "There is power in silence, confidence, and persistence." We don't have to look any further than some of our favorite fictional TV characters to see the juxtaposition of the "strong silent type" and the more boisterous bravado often associated with swagger. Take

Mad Men's Don Draper, played brilliantly by actor Jon Hamm. He doesn't need to do any chest pounding or fist pumping to prove his self-assurance. He's brooding and somewhat mysterious, but he oozes cool, and he's got swagger to spare. (We know this because he gets all the girls!)

On the other end of the swagger spectrum is the character Ari Gold, from HBO's *Entourage*. The uber-agent and Hollywood power broker played by Jeremy Piven is said to be based on real-life mogul Ari Emanuel, one of the most powerful people in the entertainment industry.

Ari Gold is bold, brash, loud, and often obnoxious—yet somehow lovable at the same time. He is the personification of swagger and the picture of charisma. The character is as "ballsy" as they come. His bravado may be over the top, but you can't argue with the character's success on the show, and you can't deny the remarkable power and influence that the real-life Ari Emanuel wields.

If you think charisma doesn't translate to power, consider the fact that Ari's brother is Rahm Emanuel, former Obama chief of staff and mayor of Chicago. Swagger runs in the family!

A while back, Ari Emanuel listed his "Six Lessons" he lives by on his LinkedIn page, and those lessons are definitely worth reading. The lessons offer a glimpse into a man who has succeeded, as described in the UK's *The Independent*, by the "sheer force of his blistering personality."

WHEN THE GOING GETS TOUGH, THE TOUGH STEP UP!

Leaders are trained to lead, but the true test of leadership comes in times of challenge. I don't care how much swagger or self-confidence you have, you're going to be battle tested—and those trials will either make you or break you.

As I mentioned in chapter one, we had one of those defining moments during Super Bowl XLIX. We've been in the ticket business for twenty-five years, and I'd never seen anything like the demand for these tickets. At one point, tickets for the big game were going for $10,000! So, as a ticket broker and marketplace, you can imagine how crazy it was.

Then, just four days before the game, even as our clients were already on their way to Phoenix, our suppliers called and said they couldn't come up with tickets we had already sold. We had over a hundred seats not being delivered. Obviously, we're responsible to those clients we committed to, so we started scrambling and doing everything we could to replace those tickets.

This was a very bad situation and the first time in the history of the company that we couldn't deliver. We even had one client who had apparently sold his tickets to some drug dealers in Mexico, and they threatened to kill him if he didn't come through with their tickets! This is like crazy stuff you only see in the movies, but we were right in the middle of it!

The very first thing we did was get on the phone with the clients who were expecting their tickets, and we were very honest and up front with them. These are folks who had flights booked and hotels reserved, and we had to tell them to hold off on going since we weren't sure we were going to get their seats. We did our best to face the debacle straight on and be as proactive as possible.

We really had to meet this head-on, not only because of the obvious customer service issues, but with the press and social media, it had the potential to be a real PR nightmare. A company like ours lives or dies because of its reputation and, in this day and age, it only takes a couple of bad tweets to destroy twenty-five years of work. So, we knew we had to face the music and we knew we had to go to extraordinary lengths to make it up to our clients.

Not only did we give those customers a full refund on their tickets, but we also gave them an additional $2,000 per ticket just as a way to offset their travel costs. Then we arranged a big "make-good" party for all those clients who had made the trip, and gave them all the food they could eat and all the drinks they could drink.

We knew it would be a little awkward to invite people to a party when they didn't get their Super Bowl seats, but we wanted to meet these folks face-to-face and apologize and do our best to make it up to them. You can imagine how upset people were during this whole ordeal. I was sitting there taking the brunt of everything, meeting the people one on one, but then we went on to the party and people had the best time.

I think these folks really appreciated the fact that we didn't try to hide from this situation or pass the buck. On the contrary, we invited them to this big event and met them face-to-face. The truth is that you don't really get to be intimate with your customers unless there is a devastating situation. We always think we have great customer service, but the real test and the real intimacy actually come along when you have to face up to very difficult circumstances.

I like to call that Super Bowl ticket disaster "the worst best experience of my life," because a lot of good, strong relationships came out of the adversity. You can build customer loyalty just by doing the right thing, staying focused, and not getting distracted. We're making a genuine effort to begin to win back their trust, and it won't end with the Super Bowl—we'll make sure we take care of these clients when the next Super Bowl rolls around.

Swagger doesn't mean you stay up in the ivory tower looking down at everyone. It means being accessible and being front and center. Getting some face time with your clients, even when they're not happy with you. Dealing with problems head-on.

One thing I know about all great CEOs is that they are responsive. They get back to people. They return calls and emails. They are excellent communicators. After all, it's easy to have great relationships in the good times, but it's how you behave in the tough times that really builds the strong, lasting relationships.

SWAGGER SUCCESS STORY

FRANCIS ALBERT SINATRA

The Voice. Ol' Blue Eyes. The Chairman of the Board. The Sultan of Swoon. He was known by many names, but there was only one Frank Sinatra. And he was the epitome of swagger. The embodiment of charisma. Few people in history possessed more charm, more magnetism, and more style. What can you say about a true legend that hasn't been said a thousand times before?

Well, for one thing, he had swagger. This rough-and-tumble crooner from Hoboken, New Jersey, didn't take any crap from anyone. He was a man's man. (And a lady's man, for that matter!) One of my favorite sayings I've seen about Sinatra was "It's Frank's world. We just live in it."

Of course, Sinatra's been profiled a million times, but rumor has it that his favorite introduction was actually made by U2's Bono, who presented Frank with the Legend Award at the 1994 Grammys. Bono welcomed Sinatra to the stage and introduced him as "The chairman of the bad attitude . . . Rock 'n' roll plays at being tough, but this guy is the boss—the chairman of boss . . . I'm not going to mess with him, are you?" According to Frank's last wife, Barbara, Frank hated being called "The Chairman of the Board."

Here's a guy who, at the age of fifty-one, marries Mia Farrow, who at twenty-one is thirty years his junior. Then when his "old lady" refuses to stop shooting *Rosemary's Baby* to appear in one of his films, he serves her with divorce papers right on the set of her movie. That's gutsy, if not coldhearted. With Sinatra, it was definitely "his way" or the highway!

Sinatra associated with presidents and mobsters, fraternized with celebrities and statesmen, and was equally comfortable whether he was in Vegas with the Rat Pack or having dinner at the White House. Frank was never afraid to throw his weight around, and his hot temper got him into trouble on several occasions. He was a hell-raiser even in high school, and was expelled because of his rowdy conduct. He never graduated from high school but began singing professionally as a teenager. He learned music by ear and never learned how to read music.

Later in his career Sinatra punched out a Hollywood columnist who was critical of him, and he got into numerous scuffles throughout his heyday. He was so fond of Jack Daniels that he was buried with a bottle. And talk about power? It's widely rumored that Sinatra enlisted his mob friends to help swing the election for JFK. As Frank himself said, in his own inimitable way, "The big lesson in life, baby, is never be scared of anyone or anything."

But toughness and power alone don't give you swagger. You also need to walk the walk and have your own approach to life. No one can deny that Frank had his own style and was truly one of a kind. The singer/actor/humanitarian won eleven Grammys, an Oscar, and scores of lifetime achievement awards, including the Presidential Medal of Freedom from President (and Sinatra pal) Ronald Reagan. Oh, and he sold over 150 million records worldwide, making him one of the best-selling artists of all time.

What business and life lessons can we take from Sinatra's remarkable career?

- **Do it "your way"**—One of Sinatra's signature songs was "My Way," which is no surprise, because he truly lived the lyrics. There's no doubt that Sinatra did everything his way, almost to a fault. This is what made him an icon who will never be forgotten. You can lead, you can follow, or you can get out of the way! I suggest you lead, be your own person, and do things your way.

- **Never compromise**—Sinatra never compromised when it came to his craft. As he said himself: "Throughout my career, if I have done anything, I have paid attention to every note and every word I sing—if I respect the song. If I cannot project this to a listener, I fail. When I sing, I believe." You've got to know when to take a stand, and when to stand firm. Frank was also years ahead of his time in terms of civil rights and equality issues. You, too, can live your principles.
- **Be the "chairman" of You, Inc.**—Once he hit it big, Frank Sinatra controlled every aspect of his career. He was intentional, and he knew how to live his "brand," long before branding was a buzzword. Some may call it "controlling" or micromanaging, but when it comes to your career, if you don't control it, someone else will!
- **Be resilient**—Sinatra had more than his share of ups and downs but always managed to bounce back even better than before. When his singing career waned in the late '40s, he came back with an Oscar-winning performance in *From Here to Eternity* in 1953. Frank seemed able to reinvent himself and remain relevant in each passing decade of his long, illustrious career. He even retired in 1971, only to come roaring back out of retirement in 1974 with "The Main Event" performance at Madison Square Garden. This guy knew how to make a

comeback! Frank once said: "Don't hide your scars. They make you who you are." What can you do to reinvent yourself when you hit a rough patch? How can you be resilient and bounce back? Resiliency is a crucial quality to develop if you're going to survive in an ever-changing, hyper-competitive workplace.

- **Own your brilliance**—Frank once quipped: "I am a thing of beauty." He wasn't afraid to own his brilliance and use his God-given talents to their full potential. You don't need to be cocky or arrogant to own your brilliance. Believe in yourself. Embrace your talents, your gifts, and your uniqueness. Be the best you can be!

3

COMMITMENT

"Commitment is what transforms a promise into reality."

—Abraham Lincoln

Charisma will carry you far but, at the end of the day, it takes more than just charisma alone to truly succeed at work and life. Sure, Sinatra had swagger to spare, but he also had ambition, commitment to his craft, and an abundance of raw talent.

Charisma without commitment is just bluster or showboating—it's an empty promise. You've got to be able to back up your swagger with skills. You've got to travel the path to mastery, and that requires commitment. Serious commitment. I mean the kind of dedication needed to constantly improve, combined with an almost stubborn determination and refusal to compromise.

Commitment means setting goals and making promises—starting with the promises you make to yourself! And those can be the hardest promises to keep. Commitment begins within. It starts with being faithful to yourself and holding yourself accountable.

Commitment starts with discipline and that, too, begins internally. Self-discipline is just as important as self-confidence. It's the ability to stick with it long after that nagging little voice inside your head tells you to give up. It's about doing what's right, instead of what's convenient, and it's about how you behave when no one is watching. (By the way, these days someone is always watching! If you don't believe me, just ask the celebrities who get caught on camera at the most inopportune times!)

Five Ways to Keep Commitments

- **Make reasonable promises; then over-deliver.** It's much better to under-promise and over-deliver than it is to make promises you can't keep. Success is based on making commitments and keeping commitments, so make reasonable, reachable promises, then do more than promised.

- **Make your promises public.** If you make your commitment in a public forum, such as Facebook, then it's going to be tough to get away with coming up short.

When you go public with your promises, the public will keep you accountable!

- **Make it too painful to fail.** If you make failure unbearable, you'll have a much better chance at success. I've heard the story of people making a diet bet, for instance. They publicly state that if they do not reach their goal, they'll write a thousand-dollar check to some organization they despise, like the KKK. The thought of actually writing a check to something that goes against every fiber of your being will motivate you to keep your promise or reach your goal!

- **Put it in writing.** There's nothing more powerful than the written word, so put your promise down in writing. It's like making a contract with yourself, and no one wants to violate a contract!

- **Realize that your reputation is at stake.** Your "word" matters. Keeping your word is a sacred act, and at the end of the day, your reputation is all you've got, so never risk it.

As racing legend Mario Andretti once said, "Desire is the key to motivation, but it's determination and commitment to an unrelenting pursuit of your goal—a commitment to excellence—that will enable you to attain the success you seek."

It's so important for your own self-esteem and for your

reputation in general to finish what you start. A lot of people talk about finishing strong, but really the focus should be on just finishing.

The person who crosses the finish line at the Boston Marathon four or five hours later than the winner should be just as proud, because they finished. They did what they set out to do. They found a way to get it done. You see stories of runners literally crawling across the finish line, physically and mentally exhausted, but they still finished. That's commitment, grit, and determination.

Having done a couple of triathlons myself, I feel a lot of empathy and respect for folks who finish despite the challenges. I pulled a calf muscle halfway through one of my triathlons and had to walk the rest of the way, but I wasn't going to quit. I may not have finished strong, but I finished!

Then there are those who take commitment to a heroic level. One such example is Texas football legend Freddie Joe Steinmark. Freddie was a University of Texas defensive back who won a national championship in 1969 but succumbed to bone cancer just two years later. His actions both on and off the field made him a national symbol of courage, determination, and grit.

Steinmark's tale is the stuff of sports lore, so it's no surprise that his story has become a Hollywood movie, *My All-American*. Steinmark was an underdog in every sense of the word—considered too small to play college ball, not a single big-time football program recruited the 150-pound athlete, until legendary Texas coach Darrell K. Royal took a chance on him.

Freddie had been a standout in high school, and in his senior year he received the Golden Helmet Award from the *Denver Post* as the outstanding scholar-athlete in Colorado. Despite his small size, in 1967 he earned a football scholarship to the University of Texas at Austin under Coach Royal.

Freddie played defensive back on the freshman team and started in that position on the varsity squad during his sophomore and junior years. He was the team's leading punt returner and was named an All-Southwest Conference athlete-scholar as a sophomore. That year, the Longhorns won the Cotton Bowl and finished as the third-ranked team in the national AP Poll.

As his junior year began, Texas was touted as a possible national champion and started racking up wins. However, Freddie had developed a limp and concerned coaches were keeping an eye on him. Trainers initially diagnosed the injury as a charley horse, and Freddie played through the pain and limped his way through the season.

In December 1969, number-two-ranked Texas met the top-ranked Arkansas team in a much-anticipated and nationally televised game at Razorback Stadium in Fayetteville, Arkansas. Even President Nixon was in attendance at the game that became known as "The Big Shootout." Arkansas had built up a fourteen-point lead after three quarters, but Steinmark and the Horns roared back with a late game comeback for the 15-14 win and the national title.

A few days later, Freddie finally admitted to Coach Royal how much pain he was in, and Royal sent the scrappy safety for X-rays. The tests revealed that Freddie had played most of the season with almost an inch of his femur devoured by cancer. His leg would have to be amputated at the hip.

Amazingly, he was up and walking on crutches within a few days of the operation, and he even made it to the team's Cotton Bowl appearance against Notre Dame. He made his way to the sidelines on one leg and watched his team rally to defeat the Fighting Irish. Freddie gained national recognition for his determination and stamina and became an inspiration to his team, as well as to thousands of cancer victims.

Later, Freddie and Coach Royal met with President Nixon at the White House to mark the annual education and fund-raising drive of the American Cancer Society. Steinmark received a special citation from the president for his "steadfast faith in God, his country and himself." Freddie's story had become a national sensation.

In spite of aggressive treatment, Freddie's condition worsened, and he lost his battle with cancer in June 1971 at age twenty-two. His funeral in Denver drew the largest crowd ever in the history of Colorado, as he had become a national symbol of courage and commitment.

Today, Freddie Steinmark remains one of the most loved and admired heroes in Texas football history. When Longhorns players enter their home games today, they touch the two large photos of Steinmark that adorn the walls of the tunnel leading to the field at Darrell K. Royal Texas Memorial Stadium in Austin. It's one of the university's most revered and respected traditions. Longtime Texas Head Coach Mack Brown remarked that Freddie is still remembered, "Not necessarily for what he did, although he was a fine player, but for who he was."

And now, forty-five years later, the Freddie Steinmark story has been told in the film *My All-American*, which debuted in 2015. The story was in the making for decades but struggled to reach the big screen. That is, until another University of Texas alum, Bud Brigham, stepped in and raised the money independently, sidestepping the Hollywood studio route.

Bud is an energy entrepreneur and investor who personifies a kind of "quiet confident" swagger. Bud is as authentic and humble as they come. He has quietly used his resources to help and honor things he is passionate about, and making the Steinmark story into a movie is just one example. "There's so much texture and richness in this," Brigham says. "This film will not be 'based on a true story'—this will be a true story. That's important to us."

The movie stars Aaron Eckhart as legendary Coach Darrell K. Royal, and newcomer Finn Wittrock as Freddie Steinmark. The film was written and directed by Angelo Pizzo, who is known for other inspirational classic sports movies, such as *Rudy* and *Hoosiers*.

But as University of Texas film professor and historian Charles Ramirez Berg points out, what makes a sports movie successful is less about the action on the field and more about universal themes. "The best sports movies aren't about sports," says Berg. "They're about other things: sacrifice, determination, and the will to win." In other words: commitment. I'm proud of my friend (and tennis partner) Bud Brigham for making this movie possible.

Freddie's story still resonates all these years later because we can all relate to the grit and commitment he showed.

Whether it was defying the odds and making the team even after being told he was too small to play in college, or when playing through excruciating pain in a key game, Freddie showed what courage and determination is all about.

It's that "never quit" attitude, and the ability to keep getting up no matter how many times you're knocked down. It's showing up . . . and stepping up. I remember being on the high school tennis team, and being stung in the face by a wasp right before a key match. I was allergic, so my face puffed up like a balloon, and one of my eyes was so swollen that I could hardly see. I played the match with one eye—not because I had to, but because I was raised to show up and meet my commitments.

Commitment also requires staying power. So, while we're on the subject of sports, let's give a nod to another "swaggerlicious" sports figure, Chris "Boomer" Berman. The longtime sportscaster is the face of ESPN, where he's worked for thirty-five years—since ESPN's inception!

Berman is considered a legend in the industry, having been recognized by the Pro Football Hall of Fame and, more recently, the Cable TV Hall of Fame. He's earned National Sportscaster of the Year honors six times, and has won ten Emmy Awards and a dozen CableACE Awards.

Boomer's incredible career and longevity (in an industry where staying power is rare) is a tribute to his style and personality. He is known for his catchphrases and use of nicknames to describe players, like the NFL's Andre "Bad Moon" Rison and Roberto "Remember the" Alomar.

With his trademark combination of genuine enthusiasm,

knowledge, and humor, he has come to embody ESPN. He's best known for his signature delivery of highlights in every sport, including one of his football catchphrases, "He could . . . go . . . all . . . the . . . way!" Berman is clearly one of the most beloved and respected personalities in sports broadcasting.

There are few people who can match the success and staying power of a thirty-five-year career, let alone three and a half decades at the same network. His longevity is a testament to loving what you do and having fun doing it, and with a nickname like "Boomer," you know the guy must have swagger!

BRIGHT-SHINY-OBJECT SYNDROME

Tony Robbins once said: "One reason so few of us achieve what we truly want is that we never direct our focus; we never concentrate our power. Most people dabble their way through life, never deciding to master anything in particular."

You can't have swagger and be successful if you're a dabbler. Dabblers move from one thing to the next and get caught up in the latest bright, shiny object. Dabblers try to be jacks-of-all-trades, so they end up being masters of none. When you lose your focus, you lose your edge; you take your eye off the ball, so you swing and miss.

It's not easy to maintain focus in a world full of distractions. There's so much noise, it's easy to get sidetracked. Commitment requires focus. You have to have a laser focus and an obsessive concentration in order to nail the task at hand. That's especially difficult for entrepreneurs and creatives, who tend to come up with new ideas all the time.

It's so important—yet increasingly challenging—to be fully present. In an age when everyone is multitasking and buried in their phones, giving someone your complete, undivided attention is a sign of true respect. Being present demonstrates your character and enhances your charisma.

Being present is said to be one of the key qualities that make former President Bill Clinton so charismatic. Those who have spent time with Clinton say that when you talk to him, he has the uncanny ability to make you feel like you're the only person in the room. When you focus on the person you're with and make them feel like the center of the universe, you dramatically increase your own swagger factor.

There's a great anecdote about two powerful British rivals that illustrates the power of attention: Benjamin Disraeli became a member of the Parliament of Great Britain at the age of thirty-three, during the reign of Queen Victoria. Disraeli's main political rival was William Gladstone, a four-time Liberal prime minister who was renowned for his abilities as a speaker. In 1886, Gladstone faced off against Disraeli for the UK's prime minister post.

One evening, Mr. Gladstone took a young woman out to dinner. The following evening, the same woman had dinner with Mr. Disraeli. Asked later what impressions the two distinguished men had made upon her, she replied, "After dining with Mr. Gladstone, I thought he was the cleverest person in England, but after dining with Mr. Disraeli, I thought I was the cleverest person in England."

I make it a point to take new employees to a one-on-one lunch to spend time with them and really focus on them as an individual. I want to know what's going on in their life and be totally present with them. This means prying myself away from my mobile phone and shutting out any other distractions. But, if you can master the art of being truly present with someone, then you've given that person the rare gift of attention.

Unfortunately, focus is becoming a lost art. A 2010 study by Harvard University found that people spend 46.9% of their waking hours thinking about something other than what they're doing. The Harvard study also concluded that this mind wandering typically makes people less happy. This "condition" is so common that it's even been given its own name: CPA, or "continuous partial attention." The phrase was coined by writer and former Apple employee Linda Stone, who describes it as "the process of paying simultaneous attention to a number of sources of incoming information, but at a superficial level."

When focus and presence are practiced, the results can be significant. Steve Jobs at Apple was a real master when it came to focus. Jobs admitted, "That's been one of my mantras—focus and simplicity. Simple can be harder than complex: You have to work hard to get your thinking clean to make it simple. But it's worth it in the end because once you get there, you can move mountains."

On a similar note, Starbucks CEO Howard Schultz says: "When you're surrounded by people who share a passionate commitment around a common purpose, anything is possible." With so many things vying for our attention, focus can be extremely difficult, but as you look at the massive success of companies like Apple and Starbucks, you'll see that they owe much, if not all, of their success to that single-mindedness.

Elite athletes are another excellent example of the value of focus and commitment. We hear stories of Olympic athletes who train hours and hours a day, month after month, year after year. To achieve excellence in their sport, they've got to have an unwavering commitment and incredible dedication.

SWAGGER SUCCESS STORY

"ROWDY" RONDA ROUSEY

She is nearly undefeated in MMA (mixed martial arts). She is the former UFC Women's Champion. She's the first American to ever earn an Olympic medal in judo, and she's widely considered to be the best in the world in her sport. She's Ronda Rousey, and she's got talent, dedication, and swagger to spare.

Rousey began taking judo lessons with her mother at the age of eleven. Her mother, AnnMaria De Mars, had enjoyed a successful judo career and was the first American to win a World Judo Championship in 1984. (Proving that the apple doesn't fall too far from the tree!)

Ironically, Ronda didn't discover that her mom had been a judo champion until she was eight. That same year, her beloved father and namesake, Ron, committed suicide. While the tragic event shook Ronda's world, discovering that her mother had been a world champion inspired her to take up judo. "It was an unbelievable discovery as a kid," admits Rousey. "All this time, I'd been looking at my dad as big, strong, invincible, and my mom as the nurturer. I had no idea that my mom could kick my dad's ass."

Her mother taught Ronda the importance of discipline and commitment. "My first injury ever was a broken toe," Ronda recalls, "and my mother made me run laps around the mat for the rest of the night. She said she wanted me to know that even if I was hurt, I was still fine." Her mom also used to tell her: "You're not training to be the best in the world, you're training to be the best in the world on your worst day."

All that training and discipline paid off. By the age of seventeen, Ronda had qualified for the 2004 Olympic Games in Athens, becoming the youngest judoka in the entire games. In 2004, she won a gold medal at the 2004 World Junior Judo Championships in Hungary. In 2008, Rousey competed at the Beijing Olympics, where she won a bronze medal. With that victory, Rousey became the first American to win an Olympic medal in women's judo since its inception as an Olympic sport in 1992.

In a recent profile in the *New York Post*, journalist Maureen Callahan writes: "She's been called a 'slaughterhouse in a blouse'—by Eminem, no less—and loves it. She can take all comers, male or female, and was just ranked the No. 1 pound-for-pound MMA fighter by *Sports Illustrated*. She usually puts someone away in under a minute; one recent fight was 14 seconds."

Callahan points out that "Rousey has also made *Maxim*'s Hot 100 list and *Forbes* magazine's 30 Under 30. She was just named the Most Dominant Athlete Alive by *Business Insider*, beating out LeBron James."

It wasn't a smooth ride to the top for Rousey. After her father's death, she dropped out of school to train for the 2004 Olympics. She placed ninth that year, and returned home exhausted and depressed. Even after she took the bronze medal in the 2008 Olympics, her life was rocky. At one point, she had started smoking and drinking and was sleeping in her car.

Then one day, when working as a bartender in Los Angeles, Rousey spotted an MMA fight on the TV above the bar. It turned out to be a watershed moment for her. "I could totally do that," she thought.

Her first MMA fight lasted just 23 seconds. "I felt a level of joy that I had never experienced before," says Rousey of her first MMA victory. Her patented "arm bar," an extremely difficult judo move that she has perfected, is enough to defeat any opponent.

Having dominated the MMA world, Rousey has since expanded into the UFC (Ultimate Fighting Championship) and WWE (World Wrestling Entertainment). Rousey has become a mainstream celebrity, with movie appearances, magazine covers, sponsorships, and endorsements.

Even with her first and only recent UFC defeat at the hands of Holly Holm, there's no doubt that Rousey will come roaring back.

Does Rowdy Ronda have swagger? If you ask her, she says: "Some people like to call me cocky or arrogant. But I just think 'How dare you assume I should think less of myself.'"

4

COURAGE

"Courage is being scared to death . . .
and saddling up anyway."
—John Wayne

What does courage have to do with swagger? Just about everything! Being courageous goes hand in hand with commitment, charisma, and confidence.

In the previous chapter, we learned why MMA fighter Ronda Rousey is another great example of a person with swagger. Rousey is clearly someone with a great deal of courage but, ironically, she admits to often feeling scared: "People say to me all the time, 'You have no fear.' I tell them, 'No, that's not true. I'm scared all the time. You have to have fear in order to have courage. I'm a courageous person because I'm a scared person.'"

Nelson Mandela said it even more eloquently when he stated: "I learned that courage was not the absence of fear, but the triumph over it. The brave man is not he who does not feel afraid, but he who conquers that fear."

Having courage does not mean never being afraid. Courage is being afraid and forging ahead anyway—despite any fear. Courage is setting "stretch" goals and pushing past your limits. Courage is doing what's right instead of what's convenient. Best of all, courage gives you swagger!

If you want to be more courageous, you need only act more courageous. When you do the thing you fear, the fear disappears. Courage is like a muscle that gets stronger the more it's tested. It's about living outside your comfort zone.

However, being fearless is not the same as being reckless. It's one thing to face down your fears and be willing to take risks, but being foolish or irresponsible does not prove that you're courageous—it only proves that you're crazy!

Courage is often likened to bravery and valor—qualities that we don't see or hear about much these days. Valor sounds like a thing of the past, when gallant knights or brave gladiators fought for a cause bigger than themselves. Yet, didn't more modern-day heroes, like Gandhi or Martin Luther King Jr. or even Rosa Parks, show valor and bravery in their acts of defiance?

Fortunately, you don't have to heroically rush off into an epic battle or slay fire-breathing dragons to be courageous. You can display courage in small, but meaningful, day-to-day acts, whether it's making a tough, unpopular decision because you know it's the right thing to do . . . or taking a calculated risk when others are not willing to take the chance. Courage is about stepping up and standing firm.

Keep in mind that if you want to exemplify courage, you can't be wishy-washy or indecisive. You've got to be intentional and committed. You've got to have the "courage of your convictions." You also need to be able to trust yourself. Intuition is a quality that is often overlooked. Stop second-guessing yourself and go with your gut. Business titan and presidential candidate Carly Fiorina says: "You have to master not only the art of listening to your head, you must also master listening to your heart and listening to your gut."

With that in mind, here are seven quick tips for calling up your courage:

1. **Accept the fear**—"Feel the fear and do it anyway" is a common refrain. Fear is a natural emotion, even if it seems irrational at times. If you find yourself gripped by fear, start by accepting it—even embracing it! Once you've come to terms with the emotion, don't allow it to envelop you. Simply accept it and move on.
2. **Get outside your comfort zone**—Once you've learned to accept fear, you can go one step further and actually invite it! Push the boundaries of your comfort zone and force yourself to do new, scary, and uncomfortable things. The only way to be fearless is to constantly push yourself.

3. **Make bold declarations and deliver on them**—Fortune favors the bold, so make daring, audacious statements and then stand by them. When you make bold declarations—and deliver on them—you become more confident and courageous. As author Robert Kiyosaki points out, "Often, in real life, it's not the smart that get ahead, but the bold."

4. **Test your limits**—Push beyond your limits and constantly test your boundaries. Exercise your courage muscles by going over and above what you "think" you can do. Remember the famous Henry Ford quote: "Whether you think you can or you can't, you're right!"

5. **Do the thing you fear most**—Do that which you fear, and the fear disappears. Action cures fear. You've probably heard it said that FEAR is an acronym for "False Evidence Appearing Real." (Others might argue that fear stands for "Forget Everything and Run"!) Either way, by doing the very thing you fear, you render fear powerless. You win!

6. **Share your fears**—When we internalize fear, we give it power over us. But when we share our fears, they dissipate. "Phone a friend" and share what you're afraid of. Chances are good that you'll feel better just having stated your fear out loud. As a bonus, your friend may help you alleviate your fears.

7. **Realize that "this too shall pass"**—You can also get philosophical about your fears and put them into context.

> "This too shall pass" is an ancient adage that loosely translates to "nothing endures." Ask yourself, "What's the bigger picture? What's the worst that can happen?" Then consider the old saying that, no matter the situation, time will pass and all things will change.

If you need a fictional, but fun, example of taking courage and swagger to the next level, look no further than the *Entourage* television and movie persona of Ari Gold. Here's a look at developing more courage and chutzpah by asking the burning question "What Would Ari Gold Do?"

WWAGD: "WHAT WOULD ARI GOLD DO?"

Ari Gold is the fictional uber-agent and star of HBO's *Entourage* series, which was also a feature film. Gold is played to perfection by Jeremy Piven, who gives the character his brash, over-the-top, but somehow lovable persona.

Ari is said to be modeled after real-life Hollywood power broker Ari Emanuel, one of the most powerful (and colorful) men in the entertainment industry. Both the TV Ari and the actual Ari can be bold, unapologetic, and downright obnoxious, but there's no denying their success or swagger.

The lines between fiction and reality are often blurred on *Entourage*, with real-life celebrities playing themselves and making numerous cameos. To make matters more sublimely fuzzy, Ari Gold has a business book out called *The Gold Standard: Rules to Rule By*.

In it, he outlines eighteen sometimes brilliant, often ruthless "rules" for gaining power and achieving total domination. Among the more practical of Gold's guidelines are "You Don't Have Any Power Until You Have All the Power," "Your Most Important Product Is Heat," and simply "Be Everywhere."

In "Rule #2, Happiness Can't Buy Money," Gold explains in colorful language and with brutal honesty, that "Money is a resource that makes it easier for you to find your purpose and achieve your goals, not because you are buying happiness but because you are eliminating the desperation that drains happiness and distracts you from your purpose." Not bad for a fictional character!

He continues: "Loving your work doesn't mean finding a job you can tolerate for eight hours a day, but rather a job that gets you flying out of bed in the morning like a Jack Russell who just had a firecracker stuffed up his a**."

Ari's amusing, if not astute, wisdom can be used as a template for just about any business scenario. So, to piggyback on Gold's *Rules to Rule By*, here are a few more hardnosed guidelines to be more "Golden":

- **Any meeting they can't start without you is a meeting worth attending.** This tidbit is actually from Kevin Spacey's boss-from-hell character, Buddy Ackerman, in 1994's *Swimming with Sharks*. This fits in perfectly here, as Buddy was another infamous entertainment business ball-breaker, not unlike our friend Ari.

- **Extreme problems often require extreme solutions.** This ancient Italian adage is often attributed, not surprisingly, to the Mafia. This seems appropriate, as Ari Gold proudly boasts how he runs his company like the Mob. He says in his book, "I have always run my business like a Mafia Don. I look for people who are tough, ambitious and loyal, and I give them the opportunity to show me that they deserve a spot in the family."

- **Make your punishment swift and show no mercy.** Niccolo Machiavelli, philosopher and author of *The Prince*, said: "If an injury has to be done to a man it should be so severe that his vengeance need not be feared." Ari Gold has no doubt studied Machiavelli closely, as Gold is notorious for squashing his enemies like a bug.

- **Choose your battles carefully.** You can't fight every battle effectively. You need to pick and choose. As Sun Tzu reminds us in *The Art of War*: "He who knows when he can fight and when he cannot, will be victorious." Of course, if you don't need to fight at all, Sun Tzu believes that's even better: "The supreme art of war is to subdue the enemy without fighting."

- **"Shake with your right hand, but hold a rock in your left."** We'll wrap up with a quote from another of Kevin Spacey's ruthless characters, "President" Frank Underwood. This harkens back to Teddy Roosevelt's "Speak softly and carry a big stick" philosophy, but it's a sentiment that Ari Gold would no doubt endorse—except for maybe the "speak softly" part!

You may think twice before acting as audaciously as Ari Gold, but next time you're stood up for an appointment or left hung out to dry at a meeting, you might just ask yourself: "*What would Ari do?*"

Let's say that your personality is not quite as over the top as Ari Gold's. How do you develop more courage if you're an introvert? Is it possible to be bold and daring if you're naturally quiet or shy?

If you consider the likes of Abraham Lincoln, Eleanor Roosevelt, and Mahatma Gandhi, the answer is a resounding yes. All three were quiet introverts who accomplished great things, despite—or perhaps because of—their reserved demeanor.

It's important to note that there's a difference between introversion and shyness. According to Sophia Dembling, author of *The Introvert's Way: Living a Quiet Life in a Noisy World*, shyness is a behavior in reaction to conditions, and introversion is a motivation. Natural extroverts can actually be shy. Whether introvert or extrovert, it's important to know that shyness can be overcome. "Introversion is hardwired, and there is no reason to want to overcome it," she says.

As Dembling describes it, introverts lose energy from being around people and gain energy from being alone, while extroverts are the exact opposite. "It's simply a different way of functioning in the world and no better or worse than extroversion, although we've all been told that extroversion is better," she says.

There's always been a perception that gregarious, outgoing people have an advantage in business, but it turns out that's not necessarily the case! Whatever your style, and whatever your personality, if you want to become more courageous, you're going to have to get outside your comfort zone. That may come a little less naturally if you're shy, but as long as you recognize your strengths and weaknesses, you can adapt accordingly.

For example, introverts can be quite social, but may need more "alone time" to recharge and regroup. Introverts may also have a harder time sharing their ideas and "putting themselves out there," but again, with practice and preparation, introverts can shine.

Courage comes in many forms, and when you consider the fact that so many "famous" people, like David Letterman, Michael Jordan, Bill Gates, and even Christina Aguilera, are card-carrying introverts, there's nothing that can stop you from being courageous too.

SWAGGER SUCCESS STORY

JOHN FITZGERALD KENNEDY

JFK is the first—and possibly best—example of a U.S. president who had true swagger. Yes, George Washington was a hero and the father of our country, Lincoln had a quiet dignity, Teddy Roosevelt was a rough-and-tumble "man's man," but JFK had an unmistakable and almost mysterious swagger. Whether he was facing down the Communists or hanging out with his Hollywood pals (Frank Sinatra and Marilyn Monroe being the most notorious), Kennedy had an allure and magnetism that no man before had ever brought to the White House.

Kennedy was the perfect man for the job at the right time in American history. He represented all that was good and fresh and exciting about that era: youth, hope, vitality, and an unbridled optimism. It's almost as if JFK gave the United States its swagger back.

Despite the Cold War being at its boiling point, Kennedy and the United States refused to back down from the Russians and stood firm during the Cuban Missile Crisis. This unflinching resolve only added to the Kennedy mystique. And while he had his share of failures—most notably the Bay of Pigs failed invasion of Cuba—those catastrophes did little to tarnish the Kennedy charisma.

In addition, Kennedy launched and advanced some of the most important initiatives of the century with the Space Race, the Peace Corps, and the Civil Rights Movement. It's difficult to fathom that so much was accomplished in his less than three years as president, but such was the demeanor and conviction of the Kennedy presidency. With JFK as president, there seemed to be an atmosphere of faith and hope that Americans could do the impossible—even put a man on the moon.

Kennedy was also a great orator, making him an ideal president for the early days of television and the growth of the national media. His speeches and sound bites live on and resonate more than fifty years later, giving us some of the most inspirational quotes of our generation. Perhaps he is best known for his inaugural speech, where he set the tone for his presidency with the famous "Ask not what your country can do for you, ask what you can do for your country."

QUOTABLE KENNEDY

"As we express our gratitude, we must never forget that the highest appreciation is not to utter words, but to live by them."

"The cost of freedom is always high, but Americans have always paid it and one path we shall never choose, is the path of surrender, or submission."

"Those who dare to fail miserably can achieve greatly."

"I look forward to a great future for America—a future in which our country will match its military strength with our moral restraint, its wealth with our wisdom, its power with our purpose."

"For in the final analysis, our most basic common link is that we all inhabit this small planet. We all breathe the same air. We all cherish our children's futures. And we are all mortal."

KENNEDY ON COURAGE

We've included Kennedy in the courage chapter, not only for his swagger, but because he's also the author of *Profiles in Courage*, a book he wrote in 1956 about U.S. Senators who risked their careers for their personal beliefs, for which he won the Pulitzer Prize for Biography in 1957.

Kennedy's own courage has been well documented, from his heroic rescue of his crew on the PT-109 during the Second World War, to his resolve and refusal to back down from Khrushchev and the Soviets during the Cuban Missile Crisis.

Kennedy had met with Soviet Premier Nikita Khrushchev early in his presidency in June 1961 at the Vienna Summit. The meeting between the two superpowers would prove to be a major setback for Kennedy, as it's widely acknowledged that JFK appeared weak and had been "bullied" by Khrushchev.

The Summit was only six weeks after the failed Bay of Pigs Invasion of Cuba, so relations were already strained with the Soviets. The two discussed the tense situation in Berlin, where the United States occupied West Berlin and the Soviets controlled East Berlin.

Coming out of the negotiations, Kennedy admitted that he had underestimated the Soviet leader. Kennedy later said of Khrushchev, "He beat the hell out of me," and told *New York Times* reporter James Reston it was the "worst thing in my life. He savaged me." Just a few months later, the Berlin Wall was constructed, further straining relations between the East and the West.

That was the situation when it was discovered that the Soviets were building nuclear missiles in Cuba, only ninety miles from U.S. shores. The entire confrontation played out on television worldwide and was the closest the Cold War came to escalating into a full-scale nuclear war. Kennedy's (and America's) courage and resolve would be tested, and the stakes had never been higher.

While the United States had considered many options, including air strikes or a full-scale invasion of Cuba, Kennedy opted for a naval blockade of the island, forcing a major stalemate. Whether it was Kennedy's previous experience with Khrushchev, or his own internal fortitude, the president stood firm.

After thirteen very tense days, along with secret negotiations and deliberations between the Soviet Union and Kennedy's cabinet, Kennedy secretly agreed to remove all U.S. missiles set in southern Italy and in Turkey, in exchange for Khrushchev removing all missiles in Cuba. There would also be a public declaration that the United States would never invade Cuba.

That showdown brought the world to the brink of nuclear war, but the crisis improved the image of America's willpower and that of the president. Kennedy's approval rating shot up to 77%, and the Cuban Missile Crisis helped cement his legacy.

Kennedy also displayed his courage and commitment with many groundbreaking domestic issues, which he called the "new frontier."

The ambitious initiative promised to tackle education, medical care for the elderly, economic aid to the poor, and racial discrimination.

The Civil Rights Movement was one of the most pressing issues of the Kennedy administration, and Kennedy would have to show both resolve and political finesse to advance racial integration and civil rights. In 1961, Kennedy signed an Executive Order for affirmative action, which required government contractors to "take affirmative action to ensure that applicants are employed and that employees are treated during employment without regard to their race, creed, color, or national origin."

Later in 1963, the president intervened when Alabama Governor George Wallace blocked the doorway to the University of Alabama to stop two African-American students from attending. Wallace moved aside only after being confronted by the Alabama National Guard, which had just been federalized by order of the president. That evening, Kennedy gave his famous civil rights address on national television and radio, launching his initiative for civil rights legislation—to provide equal access to public schools and other facilities, and greater protection of voting rights. After his assassination, Kennedy's proposals became part of the Civil Rights Act of 1964.

The early '60s were a tumultuous and turbulent time in American history, but John F. Kennedy demonstrated remarkable courage in the face of new and dangerous threats. From the tensions of the Cold War to the escalating conflict in Vietnam, Kennedy never shrank from his responsibilities, nor difficult decisions. Those of us in business may not have to make such grave life-and-death decisions, but we can certainly follow his example when it comes to being fearless and resolute.

On the fiftieth anniversary of JFK's assassination, President Obama paid tribute to Kennedy's courage, saying: "Fifty years later, John F. Kennedy stands for posterity as he did in life—young, and bold, and daring."

"And he stays with us in our imagination not because he left us too soon, but because he embodied the character of the people he led," Obama said. "Resilient. Resolute. Fearless and fun-loving. Defiant in the face of impossible odds and, most of all, determined to make the world anew—not settling for what is, but rather for what might be. In his idealism—his sober, square-jawed idealism—we are reminded that the power to change this country is ours."

As JFK noted: "The courage of life is often a less dramatic spectacle than the courage of a final moment; but it is no less a magnificent mixture of triumph and tragedy."

5

COOLNESS

"Maybe the coolest people are the ones who don't care about being cool."

—Steve Carell

We've seen how being courageous can bring you not only swagger, but massive success. Courage is a rare quality and an admirable goal so, if you've got it, you've got a big leg up on the competition.

Perhaps you've heard the story about Theodore Roosevelt, the twenty-sixth president of the United States: TR was a larger-than-life character—a force of nature who practically invented swagger. After the assassination of William McKinley in 1901, TR became the youngest president ever at the age of forty-two.

In 1912, when Roosevelt was campaigning to return to the White House, now as the leader of his new Progressive or "Bull Moose" Party, he was shot at close range. The bullet lodged in his chest just centimeters from his heart, after penetrating his eyeglass case and a fifty-page speech he was carrying in his jacket.

Yet, the defiant and determined Roosevelt insisted on giving his speech, despite blood seeping onto his shirt and aides urging him to get to a hospital. TR said to the crowd, "Ladies and gentlemen, I don't know whether you fully understand that I have just been shot; but it takes more than that to kill a Bull Moose." Roosevelt then spoke for ninety minutes before his aides could convince him to get to the hospital.

It's hard to say whether that's courage or sheer stubbornness, but the incident further built the Roosevelt legend and made him a hero in the eyes of the public. That kind of courage under fire (literally) certainly increases your swagger factor, and Roosevelt's "speak softly and carry a big stick" philosophy cemented his legacy as one of the great men of the last century.

Roosevelt is remembered as an exemplar of American masculinity, and as author and biographer Kathleen Dalton notes: "Today he is heralded as the architect of the modern presidency, as a world leader who boldly reshaped the office to meet the needs of the new century and redefined America's place in the world." Dalton refers to TR as "one of the most picturesque personalities who has ever enlivened the landscape."

In his own words, TR shared his daring philosophy:

> It is not the critic who counts; not the man who points out how the strong man stumbles, or where the doer of deeds could have done them better. The credit belongs to the man who is actually in the arena, whose face is marred by dust and sweat and blood; who strives valiantly; who errs, who comes short again and again, because there is no effort without error and shortcoming; but who does actually strive to do the deeds; who knows great enthusiasms, the great devotions; who spends himself in a worthy cause; who at the best knows in the end the triumph of high achievement, and who at the worst, if he fails, at least fails while daring greatly, so that his place shall never be with those cold and timid souls who neither know victory nor defeat.

As Henry Williams Brand wrote in his Roosevelt biography, TR was "the last romantic," who believed that "physical bravery was the highest virtue and war the ultimate test of bravery." Roosevelt demonstrated physical and mental courage throughout his colorful life, whether it was leading the "Rough Riders" in the Battle of San Juan Hill during the Spanish–American War in 1898, during his presidency, or during his dangerous South American expedition deep into the Amazon rain forest. French historian Serge Ricard may have summed it up best when he called Roosevelt "the ebullient apostle of the Strenuous Life."

Of course, it takes more than courage alone to "live like a lion." You need to master that most elusive, almost inexplicable, quality of "coolness." Of all the qualities that make up swagger, the "cool factor" may be the most difficult to master.

Let's face it: It's not easy to just suddenly be cool. "Coolness" can be carefully nurtured over time but, unfortunately, they don't teach it in high school! (Usually, by that age, you're either cool or you're not!) But don't despair, because even if you were not one of the cool kids in high school or beyond, you can still become cool at any age.

Many "cool cats" are well along in years but have been cool forever. Hugh Hefner certainly comes to mind, as do Clint Eastwood and Mick Jagger. Sure, they've always been cool, but they managed to stay relevant or get even better with age.

Others are late bloomers who didn't find their "cool" until later in life. George Clooney wasn't a megastar until the hit series *ER* put him on the map for good in 1994. Super-cool Samuel L. Jackson didn't "make it" until he was forty-six years old, after battling heroin and cocaine addictions. Even Gandhi didn't rise to prominence until age seventy-three.

The point is that even if you've never been considered "cool," there's still hope for you! And if you've lost your "mojo" or your cool factor has faded, we can help you get it back! Here are twelve ways to get it in gear:

A Dozen Ways to Crank Up Your Cool Factor

1. **Act with Confidence**—The first step to coolness begins with self-confidence. While some people will tell you

to "fake it 'til you make it," I suggest you simply act "as if" you are already sure of yourself. When you act with confidence, you gain more confidence. And confidence is cool!

2. **Create Demand**—If absence makes the heart grow fonder, then you'd be wise to create some demand and scarcity for yourself by not always being readily available. If you're too accessible and "always around," people may start taking you for granted. But when you're a bit more scarce, then you're almost automatically "in demand."

3. **Look the Part**—The sad truth is that most people still judge a book by its cover, so always try to look your best. It's just a fact of life that we're initially judged by our appearance. Dressing the part and looking sharp will go a long way toward making your first impression a positive one.

4. **Stay Positive**—Nobody likes a "Debbie Downer," so keep your negativity to yourself. Pessimism isn't cool, and you'll never be the life of the party if you're not upbeat and enthusiastic. If you can't stay positive, then stay home!

5. **Be Funny**—The only thing better than being positive is being humorous. If you're funny and fun to be around, people will flock to you. You'll be more popular, and people will think you're cool!

6. **Keep Your Cool**—There's a reason that having a meltdown is called "losing your cool." Because if you freak out, you immediately relinquish any coolness you had. Cool people show grace under pressure and are unflappable. As the saying goes, "Never let them see you sweat!"

7. **Associate with Cool People**—Surround yourself with positive, upbeat people who believe in you. This will not only increase your confidence, it will also make your environment much more supportive. There's an ancient proverb that says: "Tell me with who you go, and I'll tell you who you are." In other words, you're often the result of those with whom you spend the most time—so choose wisely!

8. **Stay Calm**—Composure is an admirable quality that makes you more likable and self-assured. While others may panic, you stay calm, cool, and collected. Think of fictional but legendary characters like James Bond or Don Corleone. Agent 007 is always composed even in the midst of bullets or missiles flying, while The Godfather wields his lethal power with a quiet, assured confidence.

9. **Keep Your Word**—There may be nothing cooler than making commitments and keeping those commitments. Keeping your word is a sign of respect and dignity. It means that you're a "stand-up guy" (or gal) who can be counted on.

10. **Know When to Exit**—Always leave them wanting more. Much like "going out while you're on top," knowing when to leave is a key ingredient to being cool. There's nothing worse than overstaying your welcome, so be sure to know when it's time to leave the stage. TV icons like Johnny Carson and Jerry Seinfeld left their shows at the peak of popularity.
11. **Keep Them Guessing**—Another way to leave everyone wanting more is to be a bit mysterious. You don't want to be a completely open book, so always hold a little something back to maintain a sense of secrecy. You don't have to be sneaky to be mysterious and enigmatic.
12. **Be Yourself**—More than anything else, you can't be cool if you're not authentic. The good news is that simply being yourself is cool. With genuineness and authenticity, you can create your own unique type of cool, and that may be the coolest trick of all!

SWAGGER SUCCESS STORY
GEORGE CLOONEY—THE KING OF COOL

George Clooney is the picture of cool. He's suave, sophisticated, and sexy. Clooney possesses that rare combination of box-office gold mixed with "good guy" humanitarian and activist. He's a global megastar who seems to have it all: an amazing career, a brilliant and gorgeous wife, a couple of Oscars, tremendous wealth (said to be worth $180 million), an Italian villa, and equally cool friends like Brad Pitt and Julia Roberts. He's the guy all the girls want and all the guys want to be . . .

Often described as the "sexiest man alive," Clooney is not just another pretty face. He is widely noted for his political activism and humanitarian work, and was named one of the "most influential people in the world" by *Time* magazine in 2009. His humanitarian work includes his advocacy of finding a resolution for the Darfur conflict, raising funds for natural disasters worldwide, and creating documentaries to raise awareness about international crises. He is also a member of the global think tank Council on Foreign Relations. A sworn and stubborn bachelor, Clooney finally tied the knot with human rights lawyer Amal Alamuddin in 2014 in Venice, Italy.

But the world wasn't always Clooney's oyster. Despite being born into a media family—his father was an anchorman and his aunt was the famous singer Rosemary Clooney—he had an uneventful childhood, and suffered from Bell's palsy in high school, a condition that partially paralyzes the face. That condition earned him the unenviable nickname of "Frankenstein" in high school, but fortunately the affliction later went away.

Clooney attended Northern Kentucky University and the University of Cincinnati but did not graduate from either. He was a "jock" who even tried out for the Cincinnati Reds in 1977 but didn't make the cut. He later worked as a shoe salesman, a door-to-door insurance salesman, and a construction worker.

Once in Hollywood, he had to live in a friend's walk-in closet and bicycle to auditions because he couldn't afford a car or bus fare. In 1984, he landed a role on the short-lived sitcom *E/R* (not to be confused with the series *ER*, in which he'd star a decade later), and had several smaller roles on such TV sitcoms as *The Facts of Life* and *The Golden Girls*.

Clooney's breakout role came in 1994 on the NBC medical drama *ER*, where he played Dr. Doug Ross. *ER* put Clooney on the map for good, and he began appearing in movies (including *From Dusk Till Dawn*, *Out of Sight* with Jennifer Lopez, and *The Peacemaker* with Nicole Kidman) even before he left the TV series in 1999.

After *ER*, Clooney starred in *The Perfect Storm* and *O Brother, Where Art Thou?*, and then played the lead, Danny Ocean, in *Ocean's Eleven*, a remake of the 1960 Frank Sinatra film of the same name. (Swagger runs in the Hollywood family!) He also began directing in 2002 with *Confessions of a Dangerous Mind*, and was nominated for a Best Director Oscar for *Good Night, and Good Luck*. He took home the Academy Award for Supporting Actor in *Syriana* in 2005 and won for Best Picture with *Argo* in 2012, which he co-produced. Clooney and Walt Disney are the only two people to have ever been nominated in six different Oscar categories.

As Tom Junod aptly pointed out in his 2013 *Esquire* article: "No one does the fame thing like Clooney. He floats above it even as he uses it to embellish his influence. He understands his place in the pantheon even as he remains hidden from the inquisitive lens. He's the master."

Junod continues: "What distinguishes Clooney from other famous people is that he reliably acts as you wish other famous people would act and does what you wish other famous people would do: often the right thing."

When Clooney isn't busy as an actor and activist, he takes time to have some fun at his friends' expense. A well-known prankster, Clooney extends his coolness by both playing, and occasionally being the brunt of, various pranks with his famous friends. Brad Pitt, Matt Damon, and the late producer Jerry Weintraub were frequent victims.

Here are few of the more legendary hijinks that the ever-cool Clooney has pulled on his friends:

- Clooney can do a perfect imitation of *Ocean's Eleven* producer Jerry Weintraub. Clooney used it to request a 4:30 a.m. hotel wake-up call for Weintraub. Later, when on a flight with Weintraub and Brad Pitt, they challenged Weintraub to a vodka-drinking contest. Clooney and Pitt, however, were drinking water. When Weintraub passed out, they filled his underwear with M&Ms.

- During the making of *The Monuments Men*, Matt Damon was staying with Clooney. Knowing that Damon was trying to lose weight, Clooney had a tailor take Damon's pants in an eighth of an inch every few days. Damon could not understand how he was gaining weight despite dieting.

- One of Clooney's favorite victims is the paparazzi, and in 2005, Clooney went to great lengths to dupe the press. He threw a fake wedding for Brad Pitt and Angelina Jolie by ordering high-top tables and tents, and put them on his lawn, so

> helicopters would see it. For two weeks the press believed the wedding was really happening.

Clooney is often referred to by both friends and industry titans alike as something of a "throwback." He's been called "old-school cool" and has even been dubbed a modern-day Frank Sinatra. As MSNBC writer Joseph V. Tirella writes: "These days Clooney is the closest thing we've got to Ol' Blue Eyes: an A-Lister who knows he's got it all, and isn't afraid to enjoy it."

Tirella reminds us that "Frank Sinatra wasn't just a singer who revolutionized American music. He wasn't just a pop star who became an Oscar-winning actor. Nor was he simply an artist who commanded creative control when most of his contemporaries did as they were told. For decades Sinatra defined all things cool."

The comparisons to Clooney are almost inevitable: Both were not only ladies' men, but also men's men. Clooney has assembled his own "Rat Pack" of sorts, most of whom make up his supporting cast in the *Ocean's* franchise, like Brad Pitt, Matt Damon, Don Cheadle, and Julia Roberts.

Sinatra was politically active in his day, even using his Mob connections to swing the election for JFK. Clooney has been equally savvy in politics and world affairs, using his influence to support President Barack Obama and other international causes.

Both men never forgot their humble roots: Sinatra was ever-cognizant that he was just "a kid from Hoboken," while Clooney hailed from Lexington, Kentucky, but didn't find real fame until his thirties.

What can we learn from George Clooney's success? How can we emulate this icon of cool to be more in control ourselves? Here are a few suggestions from the Clooney playbook:

- **Surround yourself with good people**—As Tom Junod points out in the *Esquire* piece, "He is the president of a club of famous people he doesn't consider a-holes, and he convenes it every time he makes a movie. He has made movies with Brad Pitt, Matt Damon, Bill Murray, John Goodman, Don Cheadle, Julia Roberts, and Cate Blanchett." Who you associate with really matters, so choose your friends wisely!

- **Choose your projects wisely**—In addition to being selective with his associates, Clooney also chooses his projects carefully. While he was starring on the TV series *ER*, he took on movie roles that kept him from being typecast as his *ER* character, like *From Dusk Till Dawn* in 1997. He even donned the cape for *Batman & Robin* in 1997, but after critics panned the film, he became even more selective about his roles. Clooney manages to skillfully walk the line by alternating big commercial films, like the *Ocean's* movies, with more artistic and risky projects, such as *Intolerable Cruelty* and *Syriana*.

- **Use your influence for the greater good**—Clooney also selects his causes carefully, and he finds a way to wield his box-office power into awareness and support for important issues such as the genocide in Darfur. He's been a guest at the White House (and President Obama has been to his house), and he's even spoken to the UN Security Council.

- **Be willing to give and take a joke**—Despite being an advocate and activist for these serious issues, Clooney is not above dishing out his share of hijinks and shenanigans. Clooney is notorious for his legendary pranks, and he's been known for going to great lengths to outsmart and out-prank his own personal Rat Pack.

- **Remember where you came from**—It took Clooney until his thirties before he enjoyed real fame, after struggling through Hollywood for years. As such, he's never forgotten his humble roots and he takes nothing for granted. As he mentions in the *Esquire* article: "I had my Aunt Rosie [singer Rosemary Clooney], who was famous and then not, so I got a lesson in fame early on and I understood how little it has to do with you and also how you could use it."

Clooney is clearly a man who is comfortable in his own coolness, without ever flaunting it. He's got swagger without the attitude—a good guy who does good things with his fame and fortune—and that's pretty cool!

6

COMPETITIVENESS

"It's nice to have valid competition.
It pushes you to do better."
—Gianni Versace

I can't imagine anyone with swagger who is not also competitive. In fact, to be confident and successful, it's absolutely crucial that you're a fearless and feisty competitor. In a crowded, competitive world, you've got to stay sharp to maintain your edge—that requires drive, determination, and persistence.

Competition lies at the heart of almost everything we do, from relationships and wealth to sports and business. We live in a culture of keeping up and "staying on top," where everything is a contest and everyone wants to win, and while competitiveness may seem more like a male trait, that goes for both men and women!

We pay professional athletes obscene amounts of money to watch them compete in a "winner take all" world. We elect our leaders in what is essentially a competition; we reward our kids in competitions; and we compete for jobs, partners, money, homes . . . For better or worse, it's all about competition—and the big winners are the most competitive.

Mental toughness is also lauded as an essential quality for success. To remain competitive and "keep pace" with others, you need to stay sharp, focused, and determined. You've got to be "in it to win it"! Much of competition is attitude, so you've got to understand what drives you so you can stay motivated.

However, being seen as "too" competitive can often have negative connotations. Ultra-competitive people are sometimes considered too assertive or aggressive. When caught up in the heat of competition, it's easy to let your passion get the best of you. This can lead to anger, jealousy, or resentment. The goal is to be competitive but not combative. When you channel that competitive energy in a positive way, it will give you a tremendous advantage. As author Simon Sinek says: "Believing that your competition is stronger and better than you pushes you to better yourselves."

Here are ten keys to becoming more competitive:

1. **Know Your Goal:** A ship without a destination is floating aimlessly, and an individual without a specific goal is just as lost at sea. If you want to compete, you've got

to be crystal clear on the prize. What is your ultimate goal? Whether you're competing in a race or vying for a promotion, you've got to know where you're trying to go! Where's the "finish line"? How will you know when you've reached it? What's the end result you're after? Any competition—work, sports, or performance—requires that you know your goal from the get-go.

2. **Know Your Opponent:** Almost as important as knowing your goal is knowing your rival. Who are you facing? What are you up against? Do you have one opponent, or many? What are your opponent's strengths and weaknesses, and how can you exploit them to your advantage? Study your competition to give yourself an edge. Information is power. As the old saying goes, "It's a jungle out there," so make sure you're well equipped for the journey.

3. **Do the Work:** This one is so obvious that not many people even talk about it. It's almost assumed that to be truly competitive, you simply have to put in the time, make the commitment, and do the work. There's no substitute and no shortcuts when it comes to hunkering down and getting it done. It's said that to achieve true mastery in any profession or endeavor, it takes over 10,000 hours of practice. The sooner you dive in and get to work, the sooner you'll be on the path to mastery.

4. **Test Your Limits:** You'll never know how far you can go until you push your limits and go beyond what you

think you are capable of. The same is true whether you're an athlete or an accountant. Of course, we often hear about "pushing past your limits" in the world of sports, but reaching beyond expectations is not just for physical challenges, but also for mental, emotional, and personal limits. Go to the edge. Then go farther!

5. **Do Your Best:** Sometimes even the most common clichés are clichés because they are so basic and true. You've always got to do your best and give it everything you've got. Anything less and you'll never find yourself in the winners' circle. When coaches say "Leave it all out there on the field," they mean you need to give every ounce of effort you possibly can. It may be a more common refrain for sports, but it's true in business, too. The best clichés ring true: Do your best.

6. **Never Settle:** In order to remain competitive and be the best, you can't settle for second best! If you want to beat your competition, "good enough" is never good enough. Don't settle for less—whether from yourself or from your team. When it comes to competition, there's no place for compromise. It's win or go home!

7. **Dig Deeper:** When you refuse to settle, it means you're going to need to dig deeper—to reach down inside and summon the strength and courage and fortitude to best the competition. Again, the sports analogies for "digging deeper" may be more common, but the same is true with anything that involves competition—physical,

mental, or otherwise. Everything you need is already inside you. Now you just need to dig deep and call it up!

8. **Respect Your Rituals:** Most elite athletes and performers have a ritual they practice before a big game or match. Olympic champion (and most-decorated medalist) Michael Phelps has a meticulous and detailed ritual that he goes through before every single swim meet. I was fortunate enough to be at the 2008 Beijing Olympics when Phelps shattered several records and won an amazing eight gold medals. According to FitDay.com, Phelps follows the same routine at every race: "He eats the same breakfast (eggs, oatmeal, and four energy shakes), works through the same stretching routine, completes the same 45-minute warm-up, and listens to hip-hop while he waits for his race to start." Rituals are more than superstitions, so do what you need to do to "get in the zone," and respect your rituals to maintain your edge.

9. **Failure Is an Option:** Life is not *Apollo 13*, where failure is not an option. In the game of life and business, failure is an option. In fact, it's inevitable. You can't compete unless you try and take risks, and your journey will always include failures—perhaps even more failures than wins. The only way to grow and improve is to fail often and learn from those failures. As tennis great Billie Jean King said: "For me, losing a tennis match isn't failure, it's research." Even the greatest baseball players of all time fail seven out of ten times. If a 300% batting

average makes you an elite ball player, imagine what it can do for you! Don't be afraid to fail!

10. **Resilience Is Key:** Perhaps more than any other quality, resilience is vital in any competitive environment. The ability to bounce back and try again is often the difference between success and failure. You will get knocked to the mat, but you must get back up! Like the proverb states: "Success is falling down seven times and getting up eight." Be resilient. Bounce back. Live to fight another day!

SWAGGER SUCCESS STORY
SIR RICHARD BRANSON

Few people epitomize swagger like Sir Richard Branson. The billionaire founder of the Virgin Group is best known for his flair, his boldness, and his sense of adventure. If swagger is about success, confidence, and innovation, Branson may very well be our finest example.

I was extremely fortunate to be a guest of Sir Richard Branson at his home on Necker Island, swimming and playing tennis, as well as going on several safaris with him at his African retreat Mahali Mzuri. I realized Branson has an amazing attribute, which is his passion to listen. This skill enhances his charm and enables him to personify swagger. Branson is also very gracious and has a desire to give credit to others by showing appreciation, humility, and gratitude.

An entrepreneur and pacesetter since the age of fifteen, Branson had launched his first venture, a magazine called *The Student*, by the time he was seventeen. His dyslexia made him a poor student, but his parents saw his potential and supported his endeavors and ambitions.

Best known for the Virgin brand, including Virgin Megastores and Virgin Atlantic Airways, the Virgin Group now comprises more than a hundred companies and employs over 60,000 people in fifty countries.

Branson started Virgin as a mail-order record business in 1970, and by 1972 he had opened the first Virgin Records retail shop in London. Having earned enough money from his record store, Branson then purchased a large country estate, where he built a recording studio called The Manor Studio. He leased the studio to fledgling artists, including instrumentalist Mike Oldfield, who had Virgin Records' first hit with *Tubular Bells*.

Virgin went on to sign controversial acts such as The Sex Pistols, and also introduced '80s bands such as Culture Club to the music world. Virgin Records eventually became the biggest independent record label in the world, even representing The Rolling Stones.

In 1984, Branson expanded his business ventures by founding Virgin Atlantic Airways, later expanding his travel industry ventures to include Virgin Australia, Virgin America, Virgin Holidays, Virgin Limited Edition, Virgin Trains, Virgin Hotels, and even Virgin Galactic, his bold space-tourism company.

When asked about his risky decision to go into the airline business, Branson said: "My interest in life comes from setting myself huge, apparently unachievable challenges and trying to rise above them . . . from the perspective of wanting to live life to the fullest, I felt that I had to attempt it."

Branson's airline business was not without challenges. In the early

'90s, Virgin accused competitor British Airways of what came to be called the "Dirty Tricks" campaign, after British Airways was suspected of poaching Virgin's passengers and even hacking into their computers. BA settled the case and was forced to pay Branson almost a million dollars—which he distributed among his staff as a "BA Bonus."

In 1992, to keep the airline afloat, Branson was forced to sell his Virgin record label to EMI for nearly $800 million. Branson admitted that he wept when the sale was completed because the record business had been the start of the Virgin empire. The defeat did little to stop Branson's expansion, as he continued to launch audacious ventures from Virgin Trains to Virgin Vodka. While not all of the businesses have been a success, Branson is the only individual to ever build eight different billion-dollar companies in eight separate sectors.

As an adventurer, Branson's endeavors are equally bold: He's made several successful world-record-breaking attempts, including the fastest ever Atlantic Ocean crossing, a hot-air-balloon Atlantic crossing, and even a kitesurfing crossing of the English Channel. Between 1995 and 1998, Branson and colleagues Per Lindstrand and Steve Fossett made several unsuccessful attempts to circumnavigate the globe by hot-air balloon. He continues to push the boundaries of adventurism with Virgin Galactic, which he plans to take into space on the first public outer-space voyage.

Branson is also a record breaker online, voted the UK's number-one Twitter user (with over 6 million followers), the world's most social CEO, and the world's most-followed person on LinkedIn. Branson also maintains a daily blog discussing everything from entrepreneurship, conservation, and sustainability to travel, music, and humor. He has more than 24 million followers across seven social platforms. He is also the author of seven books, including *The Virgin Way; Like a Virgin; Screw*

Business as Usual; Reach for the Skies; Business Stripped Bare; Screw It, Let's Do It; and his autobiography, *Losing My Virginity*.

With a net worth of $4.9 billion, Branson now spends as much as 80% of his time on humanitarian causes and philanthropy. However, Branson promoted social change long before he was wealthy. Since starting youth culture magazine *The Student*, he's been a strong supporter of social and environmental causes. At seventeen, he launched the Student Advisory Centre to assist young people with issues such as abortion and sexuality.

Today, he continues to assist young entrepreneurs through "Virgin Startup," an initiative that provides loans to entrepreneurs in the UK who are between the ages of eighteen and thirty. He's also a founding sponsor of the International Centre for Missing & Exploited Children (ICMEC), an organization set up to help find missing children and to stop the exploitation of children.

In 2004, he established the nonprofit foundation Virgin Unite to tackle difficult social and environmental problems. Many of Branson's public service initiatives fall under the Virgin Unite foundation, such as The Elders, a small but dedicated group of international leaders who use their expertise and influence "to catalyze peaceful resolutions to long-standing conflicts, articulate new approaches to global issues that are causing or may cause immense human suffering, and share wisdom by helping to connect voices all over the world." Members of The Elders have included the late Nelson Mandela, Kofi Annan, and Jimmy Carter.

Other humanitarian initiatives under the Virgin Unite banner include the Carbon War Room, founded in 2009 to seek solutions for global warming and renewable energy. Branson set up the Virgin Earth Challenge, offering a $25 million prize for scalable and sustainable ways of removing greenhouse gases from the air. He has also hosted environmental conferences and retreats with entrepreneurs and world leaders on Necker Island, his seventy-four-acre private island in the Caribbean.

Having long been influenced by Nelson Mandela, Branson continues to focus much of his philanthropy on South Africa. In 2005, he set up the Branson School of Entrepreneurship in Johannesburg to improve economic growth in South Africa by supporting start-ups with skills, mentors, services, networks, and financing. In addition, as *Forbes* magazine reports, "His safari preserve in South Africa runs a nearby clinic dispensing free anti-retrovirals and medicine for TB and malaria. His Virgin Active gym club chain in South Africa created a gym in Soweto Township with the community that houses a hair salon and other ventures, and is now one of its most profitable gyms in the country."

In 2012, Branson created the "B Team," an advocacy group of world leaders who encourage other business leaders to take a bigger stand for human rights. According to *Forbes*, "Its 17 members are a supergroup of business and political leaders with an activist bent, including Unilever CEO Paul Polman, Indian industrialist Ratan Tata, former Irish prime minister Mary Robinson, Nobel laureate Muhammad Yunus, Nigerian finance minister Ngozi Okonjo-Iweala, Tom's Shoes founder Blake Mycoskie and media entrepreneur Arianna Huffington."

As Branson shared with *Forbes*: "Up until now, businesses have thought of themselves as businesses . . . there to worry about the bottom line and create jobs, but they've been frightened about speaking up about issues. What we hope for with the B Team is for them to be a lot braver. If we see that women's rights are not being protected in certain countries, we will speak out about it. If we feel that the rights of individuals who love each other, but are of the same sex are not being protected we will speak out about it and we will do our best to use the influence we have to try to get some sense and try to change opinions."

The statement issued by the B Team at the World Economic Forum in *Davos* in 2014 serves as a mission statement not only for the group, but one that can also be used as a guide for other businesses like ours. The statement reads:

> Business has been improving people's lives for centuries, creating jobs, driving innovation and extending prosperity. Certainly business leaders do not try and cause harm to the people that work for them, but often the warped incentives we've created to drive profitability put such pressure on the organization, that we lose sight of the most important part of any company, our people. There needs to be a completely new approach to how we operate as business leaders, one that clearly puts people at the center of all we do. To do this we need to turn upside down the "old way" of doing business and create a "Plan B", focused on longer-term horizons and a goal of helping people to thrive, rather than maximizing profit at all cost.
>
> We know that much remains to be done, and the news of the past twelve months—from the widely publicized situation of migrant workers in the Gulf States to the harrowing images of the RANA plaza factory collapse in Bangladesh—are powerful reminders of the damage that can be wrought.
>
> At a minimum, businesses can start by implementing the UN's Guiding Principles on Business and Human Rights, not only in their core operations, but across their supply chain. Decent working conditions, fair wages and stable

> communities could quickly become the norm, if encouraged by ethical purchasing decisions. Business can also go further, working with governments to strengthen governance and end corruption.

Branson appears on the list of "100 Greatest Britons," and has also been included in *Time* magazine's "Top 100 Most Influential People in the World." He has also been recognized by the UK's *Sunday Times* as "the most admired business person over the last five decades."

In 1999, Queen Elizabeth announced that she would confer the honor of Knight Bachelor on him for his "services to entrepreneurship," and in 2000, he was knighted Sir Richard Branson by Prince Charles at a ceremony at Buckingham Palace.

7

CHARACTER

"A man's character is his fate."
—Heraclitus

There's a difference between having character and *being* a character! It's fine to be a "character," which essentially means that you have a fun, memorable, and unique persona. But the kind of character we're talking about here has to do with your integrity and reputation. Your character is your moral fiber and, like the other qualities discussed in this book, character is essential for personal and professional success.

I know plenty of characters—some are eccentric, others just have big personalities. However, possessing true character —that innate authenticity and veracity—is a rare and valuable quality. Your character is your temperament and spirit. It's the very essence of who you are. Having character means you do the right thing, even when no one is watching. It means you can be counted on. It means that you're a stand-up guy (or gal).

In the movie *Gladiator*, with Russell Crowe, Roman soldiers greeted each other with the phrase "Strength and Honor." While it may sound even more regal in Latin, "fortitudinem et honorem," there's no real evidence that the greeting was actually used by the ancient Romans. Still, the idea of strength and honor is something to aspire to as you develop your own character.

The 1800s politician and orator Henry Clay once said: "Of all the properties which belong to honorable men, not one is so highly prized as that of character." Character encompasses honor, truth, reliability, and reputation. It's showing moral and ethical strength under any circumstances.

Character is often associated with integrity—particularly moral integrity, as in being an "upstanding character." Sociologist James Davison Hunter wrote a book called *The Death of Character*, in which he identified the three qualities of true character as moral discipline, moral attachment, and moral autonomy. As Davison summarizes: "Character, in a classic sense, manifests itself as the autonomy to make ethical decisions always on behalf of the common good and the discipline to abide by that principle." So, character is not only what you do, but who you are.

In his book *Making Ethical Decisions*, author Michael Josephson outlines the "Six Pillars of Character" as trustworthiness, respect, responsibility, fairness, caring, and citizenship. As Josephson points out: "No one is born with good character; it's not a hereditary trait and it isn't determined by a single noble act. Character is established by conscientious adherence to moral values, not by lofty rhetoric or good intentions. Another way of saying that is, character is ethics in action."

With that in mind, here's my take on Josephson's Six Pillars of Character:

1. **Trustworthiness**—It's impossible to be a person of character if you can't be trusted. Trust is a sacred vow and, once broken, can rarely be repaired. To be trustworthy means being deserving of trust and confidence, and of course that trust must be earned. To earn trust, you must be reliable, honest, and loyal. It's a key component of any businessperson or entrepreneur. In fact, trust is one of the main things that *Shark Tank's* Daymond John looks for in an investment partner: "In the founders, I look for a person I feel is trustworthy, driven and smart," admits John. "I invest in the person first, because in the event the business fails, the person and I can move forward and create another business."

2. **Respect**—Respect is something you must show others if you expect the same in return. Everyone should be treated with decency and dignity, but self-respect is

equally important. In the words of Clint Eastwood: "Respect your efforts, respect yourself. Self-respect leads to self-discipline. When you have both firmly under your belt, that's real power."

3. **Responsibility**—Being accountable for your actions is another key to your character. Here at TicketCity, I like to say: "Give the credit. Take the blame." That means taking responsibility for all of our actions and never "throwing anyone under the bus." It also means realizing that there are always consequences, and we must always face those consequences head-on. You simply can't afford to shirk your responsibilities unless you're willing to have your character take a hit.

4. **Fairness**—Like responsibility, fairness is another crucial aspect of character building. That means we can't play favorites and everyone gets treated equally. Fairness also means admitting your mistakes and correcting them as quickly as possible. A lot of people talk about fairness, but it's got to be more than just lip service. As journalist Brit Hume reminds us: "Fairness is not an attitude, it's a professional skill that must be developed and exercised."

5. **Caring**—In the context of character, caring doesn't necessarily mean being sweet and kind, it means showing real care and concern for your fellow man. Legendary UCLA basketball coach John Wooden once said: "I worry that business leaders are more interested in

material gain than they are in having the patience to build up a strong organization, and a strong organization starts with caring for their people."

6. **Citizenship**—Josephson's final "pillar" of character is citizenship. To many, that evokes images of voting or giving back to your community. While that's certainly an important part of being a good citizen, to develop true character, you should do more than the "minimum requirements" of citizenship. Think about the different ways you might contribute more to your community. Those with character give more than they take, and they do so without regard to "payback" or personal reward.

People often confuse character and reputation. Character is who you are, while reputation is what people think you are. Character is what is deep down inside us, whereas reputation is more about image. Abraham Lincoln put it this way: "Character is like a tree and reputation like its shadow. The shadow is what we think of it; the tree is the real thing."

Aside from attempting to live these values, what can we do to "build" our character? Here are a few guidelines:

- **Do the right thing, even when you think no one is watching.** As Henry Ford put it: "Quality means doing it right when no one is looking." Real character is built by doing what's right, all the time. That means no cutting corners or taking shortcuts even when you think you can get away with it. Oh, and by the way . . . someone is ALWAYS watching. These days, cameras are absolutely everywhere. Just ask any celebrity who's been caught in a rant or any rogue cop who's been captured by a bystander's cell phone video. All the more reason to simply do the right thing.

- **Be someone who can be counted on to keep your word.** People with character are the folks who make commitments, and keep those commitments. When you make a promise, keep that promise! When you become known as someone who keeps your word, you build a solid reputation and develop more character.

- **Make swift decisions and stick to your guns.** Waffles are fine for breakfast, but "waffling" in your business and personal life is not a formula for success. Being decisive demonstrates a strong character, and sticking with your decision garners respect and admiration. As author Brian Tracy notes: "Decisiveness is a characteristic of high-performing men and women. Almost any decision is better than no decision at all."

- **Say what you mean and mean what you say.** In addition to being decisive, you must also be consistent. As Hollywood legend Robert Evans reminds us, "Don't say yes when you mean no." Be clear in your communications and say exactly what you mean to say. Call it like you see it and strive to be a straight shooter.

- **Lead by example.** Actions speak louder than words, so let your actions serve as a good example for others. As novelist and poet Oliver Goldsmith said: "You can preach a better sermon with your life than with your lips."

It's often assumed that "character" is only formed under duress, or when we're tested by great challenges. That may be one scenario when you need to muster your character, but character is also formed in everyday life, through small acts and seemingly minor decisions. Again, character is not just how you behave and what you believe, it's how you act when no one is watching. Or, as the saying goes: "It's what's inside that counts!"

German writer and statesman Johann Wolfgang von Goethe may have said it best over a hundred years ago when he said: "Character develops itself in the stream of life."

SWAGGER SUCCESS STORY

JOHN WAYNE—OLD SCHOOL SWAGGER

He was the quintessential symbol of swagger, the all-American personification of "macho," and a true cowboy who appeared in 170 movies over an amazing fifty-year career. He epitomized rough, tough masculinity, and his distinctive walk, talk, and demeanor made him an

American icon. Born Marion Robert Morrison in 1907, we know him better as John Wayne.

Wayne was born in Iowa but grew up in Southern California, where he picked up the nickname "Duke." His academic and athletic success at Glendale High School earned him a football scholarship to the University of Southern California, but a bodysurfing accident cut his college football career short.

While in college, Wayne found some work as a film extra to help pay his tuition. Once out of USC, he continued to work as an extra and prop man in the film industry. He met legendary director John Ford while working as an extra in 1928. That relationship would ultimately shape his acting career.

His first leading role came in 1930 in director Raoul Walsh's lavish widescreen epic *The Big Trail*, which led to leading roles in numerous B movies throughout the 1930s, many of them Westerns. While none of those films were breakout roles, during this time Wayne would hone his tough man-of-action persona, which would serve as the basis of many popular characters in later movies. During that first film with director Walsh, Marion Morrison would adopt the stage name John Wayne and never look back.

His movie career finally took off in 1939, with John Ford's *Stagecoach* making him an instant mainstream star. As Wayne biographer Ronald Davis points out: "John Wayne personified for millions the nation's frontier heritage. Eighty-three of his movies were Westerns, and in them he played cowboys, cavalrymen, and unconquerable loners extracted from the Republic's central creation myth."

For the next fifty years, John Wayne would continue to be one of the most enduring box-office stars. As described in his biography on the Hollywood Bowl website: "John Wayne's monumental film career spanned five decades. He appeared in more than 175 films, more than a dozen directed by John Ford alone. For an entire generation, he was Hollywood's biggest and most durable box-office star. Incredibly versatile, Wayne starred in just about every genre Hollywood offered: war movies, romantic comedies, police dramas, histories. But it was the Western—the American cinema—where Wayne made his most lasting mark. He was nominated three times for the Academy Award, winning the Oscar for Best Actor in 1969 for *True Grit.* And his powerful performance in *The Searchers* has been singled out by filmmakers and actors alike as the greatest performance by an actor on film, ever."

While many of Wayne's onscreen characters would help shape his persona, the Duke was just as iconic in real life. By the time his career was established, Wayne was careful to select movie roles that would not compromise his offscreen image. As one biographer noted: "Wayne rose beyond the typical recognition for a famous actor to that of an enduring icon who symbolized and communicated American values and ideals."

Some of his tough-guy character was undoubtedly influenced by his father and his upbringing. According to Wayne himself: "I've always followed my father's advice: he told me, first to always keep my word and, second, to never insult anybody unintentionally. If I insult you, you can be goddamn sure I intend to and third, he told me not to go around looking for trouble."

A staunch Republican and conservative, John Wayne made no bones about his stand on various issues. Early in his career, he was an ardent anti-Communist and vocal supporter of the House Un-American Activities Committee. He was also a strong supporter of the Vietnam War and helped his friend Ronald Reagan in his campaigns for governor of California.

In a controversial interview with *Playboy* magazine in 1971, Wayne pulled no punches regarding his feelings about entitlement programs like Medicare and Social Security:

> In the late Twenties, when I was a sophomore at USC, I was a socialist myself—but not when I left. The average college kid idealistically wishes everybody could have ice cream and cake for every meal, but as he gets older and gives more thought to his and his fellow man's responsibilities, he finds that it can't work out that way—that some people just won't carry their load . . . I believe in welfare—a welfare work program. I don't think a fella should be able to sit on his backside and receive welfare. I'd like to know why well-educated idiots keep apologizing for lazy and complaining people who think the world owes them a living. I'd like to know why they make excuses for cowards who spit in the faces of the police and then run behind the judicial sob sisters. I can't understand these people who carry placards to save the life of some criminal, yet have no thought for the innocent victim.

Part of John Wayne's swagger was that he made no apologies for his political stands and constantly fought for his principles. He once said, "If everything isn't black or white, I say why the hell not?" Like the movie of the same name (which won him an Oscar in 1969), John Wayne personified *True Grit*.

Shortly before his death in 1979, he was awarded the Congressional Gold Medal, one of the highest civilian decorations you can receive. The following year, Wayne was posthumously awarded the Presidential Medal of Freedom by Jimmy Carter.

John Wayne epitomized a kind of pure and powerful swagger. From his signature walk to his voice and physical presence, he was a man's man and a guy you wouldn't mess with. As Wayne himself said, "Talk low, talk slow, and don't say too much." Both onscreen and offscreen, he stood tall for what he believed in, saying, "Never apologize and never explain, it's a sign of weakness."

Despite his tough, no-nonsense image, the Duke was also a patriot and an eternal optimist. As he said: "Tomorrow is the most important thing in life. Comes into us at midnight very clean. It's perfect when it arrives and it puts itself in our hands. It hopes we've learned something from yesterday."

Above all, John Wayne had heart, character, and integrity. He was a true cowboy, a movie legend, and an American cultural icon.

8

CREATIVITY

"Creativity is piercing the mundane to find the marvelous."

—Bill Moyers

It's amazing how much confidence, charisma, and swagger you can feel when you're feeling creative. When you're creative, you're "in the zone," you're on, or you're just in the flow. The dictionary describes creativity as "the ability to transcend traditional ideas, rules, patterns, relationships, or the like, and to create meaningful new ideas, forms, methods, and interpretations."

But creativity is much more than that. It's almost a state of mind that gives you freedom, flexibility, and imagination.

Creativity is knowing that you can come up with new ways to solve old problems. It's being inventive and innovative. It's creating something completely new, different, and valuable where before there was nothing.

Steve Jobs may have captured the essence of creativity best when he said: "Creativity is just connecting things. When you ask creative people how they did something, they feel a little guilty because they didn't really do it, they just saw something. It seemed obvious to them after a while. That's because they were able to connect experiences they've had and synthesize new things."

Why is creativity so valued in the first place? Modern society greatly admires "creative" people, often likening creativity to overall intelligence and inventiveness. "Creatives" in our culture are seen as imaginative, forward-thinking problem solvers. The "creative" person is often the "go-to" guy or gal when others have failed to find an answer. They're the person everyone turns to for ideas and solutions when you're in a pinch. Creatives are seen as original, resourceful, and even inspired. Whether at home, at school, or in the workplace, creativity is synonymous with talent.

However, in our society, there's a common misconception that you're either creative or you're not. That you're just born that way—with an innate and natural "gift" of creativity. The truth is that creativity is not some genetic prize or natural talent. Like most skills, creativity can be learned, developed, and expanded. Most experts agree that we all have a wellspring of creativity, and it's really just a matter of tapping into it.

Art Markman is a PhD and professor of psychology and

marketing at my alma mater, the University of Texas at Austin. In a recent *Fast Company* article he penned about creativity, he likened creativity to a skill that can be built with practice. Markman says:

> This way of thinking about talents and skills is particularly important when it comes to thinking about creativity. For skills that involve actions in the world, such as shooting a free throw or playing a musical instrument, people have a pretty good idea of what they need to do to improve. But for mental skills like creativity, few people know enough about the way their minds work to be able to treat it like a skill.
>
> As a result, most people tend to look at those people who develop creative ideas consistently with a kind of reverence, and people who do seem blessed with a talent for creativity live in fear that talent will run out some day and they will be just like everybody else.

Fortunately, creativity can be cultivated with practice. Markman identifies three key ways to become more creative:

First, he suggests, you must "become an explainer." That means internalizing ideas so that you understand well enough to explain the idea to someone else. Next, says Markman, you need to "practice openness," or be willing to consider new ideas and new ways of thinking. Finally, you must "keep asking new questions." As Markman says: "A third critical aspect of creativity is to remember that any idea you have is something that you pulled out of your memory. That means that when you have a brilliant idea, you retrieved a helpful piece of information from memory and used it."

Still don't think you're a creative type? Here are five more ways to develop your creative muscle and become that sought-after expert:

1. **Connect the dots**—So much of creativity comes from connecting or combining two or more seemingly unrelated ideas. Don't be afraid to mix and match ideas to come up with something new. Sir Richard Branson is such a fan of "associating" that he's created an acronym at Virgin, "ABCD," for "Always Be Connecting Dots."

2. **Be willing to fail**—Most experts agree that, in order to be creative, you have to not only accept failure, but embrace it. Coming up with creative ideas is often a numbers game, and you've got to be willing to consider some "not so great" options in order to mine the golden idea.

3. **Take a hike**—If you're stuck, take a hike! Or a bike, or a walk around the block. Just get up, get out, and get a change of scenery. The change of pace will give you a new perspective, and you may see things you didn't realize before. It's also helpful to create an atmosphere that's conducive to creativity. According to Larry Kim in *Inc.* magazine's "9 Ways to Become More Creative in the Next 10 Minutes," "Google goes to great lengths to provide employees with fun perks such as beach volleyball courts and free beer, a setup almost resembling

an adult playground. The goal is to create an environment that lets employees feel relaxed and comfortable with vocalizing creative, even wacky, ideas. Businesses that value creativity need to do their best to foster a creative, safe space where unusual ideas are celebrated and where creativity is nurtured."

4. **Hit the showers**—Why is it we always seem to come up with our best ideas in the shower, or in the middle of the night? If that's the case with you, keep a notepad or voice recorder on your nightstand for those brilliant 3:00 a.m. brainstorms. What about those lightbulb moments for the shower? Believe it or not, there's even a waterproof note-taking device for the shower called "AquaNotes"!

5. **Sketch or doodle**—*Fast Company* magazine calls Sunni Brown "one of the most creative people in business." She's done a TED Talk on doodling and has written a book called *The Doodle Revolution: Unlock the Power to Think Differently*. In the book, my fellow Austin resident notes that "Some of the greatest thinkers—from Henry Ford to Steve Jobs—used doodling to jump-start creativity. Doodling can enhance recall and activate unique neurological pathways, leading to new insights and cognitive breakthroughs." And all this time you thought doodling in meetings was just a way to pass the time!

Creativity is often considered to be the same as artistic ability. We think of artists, musicians, designers, or actors as creative. We assume these "right brain" artistic types are just naturally more inventive and imaginative than the rest of us.

In truth, creativity comes in all shapes, sizes, and situations. There's creativity in business, in finances, in sports, in sales . . . No matter what your profession, you can be more creative. After all, creativity is really just a matter of looking at the world in a different way, or coming up with new or original ways of problem solving.

Apple made the phrase "Think Different" famous in their 1997 ad campaign and TV commercials that began "Here's to the crazy ones . . . "

Ironically, while the "crazy ones" copy is often attributed to Steve Jobs, much of the theme was taken from Jack Kerouac's "mad ones" quote from his *On The Road* novel. Apple's ad agency penned the actual copy for the now-famous ad campaign.

Regardless of the Kerouac debate about how the words originated, they definitely capture the essence of creativity. For the record, the "crazy ones" featured in the Apple TV commercial included Albert Einstein, Bob Dylan, Martin Luther King Jr., Richard Branson, John Lennon (with Yoko Ono), Buckminster Fuller, Thomas Edison, Muhammad Ali, Ted Turner, Maria Callas, Mahatma Gandhi, Amelia Earhart, Alfred Hitchcock, Martha Graham, Jim Henson (with Kermit the Frog), Frank Lloyd Wright, and Pablo Picasso.

Obviously, not all of these icons were artists in the true sense of the word, but you can't argue that they weren't each creative in their own way—whether it was Muhammad Ali's colorful "trash talk" or Richard Branson's innovation and flair.

This simply proves that regardless of your occupation or situation, you can stretch your creativity muscle and learn to be more innovative and inspired. You may think you're not a creative type but, just like hitting the gym to exercise your muscles, you can work your creativity muscle. In fact, according to a *Fast Company* article by Josh Linkner, creativity is a skill that can be learned and developed.

Linkner points to a study by Harvard University that says that creativity is 85% a learned skill. "That means that all of us, even on our groggy days, have 85% the creative potential as Mozart, or Picasso, or Da Vinci," says Linkner. "We simply need a process to tap into this valuable natural resource."

Linkner's *Fast Company* feature also points out the importance of creativity in the C-suite: "Creativity is the most important leadership skill for the next generation of business. According to an IBM study of 1500 CEOs creativity was ranked as the single most crucial factor for future success."

Whether you choose to enhance your creative abilities with journaling, brainstorming, doodling, hiking, or playing, you should do something every day to grow your creativity. To put it more simply, take Apple's advice and "think different"!

SWAGGER SUCCESS STORY

JIMMY FALLON—THE BOY NEXT DOOR BECOMES KING OF LATE NIGHT

Swagger comes in many forms and, yes, you can be humble, down-to-earth, and approachable, yet still have swagger. Take the relatively young and super-talented Jimmy Fallon . . .

The multifaceted (comedian, musician, actor) and effervescent Fallon has forged his own unique brand of happy-go-lucky and charming swagger. He's an easygoing everyman who came from humble roots and ascended to new heights as the king of late night and host of the venerable *Tonight Show*.

Born in Bay Ridge, Brooklyn, and raised by a middle-class family in Saugerties, New York, Fallon developed an interest in music and comedy from an early age. He loved comedy and became obsessed with *Saturday Night Live*, often reenacting their sketches with friends. Fallon began playing the guitar at thirteen, and by his teens he had earned the "class clown" label at his junior high school.

Fallon described his childhood as "idyllic," and coasted through high school as a performer in numerous stage productions and as high school social director. He attended the College of Saint Rose in Albany, New York, where his passion for comedy continued. He would often take a bus from Albany to New York City on weekends to do stand-up at Caroline's Comedy Club in Times Square. At twenty-one, he left college just one semester shy of graduating and moved to Los Angeles to pursue his comedy career.

In LA, he'd often do stand-up gigs at the Improv, earning a whopping $7.50 per set. He also joined the Groundlings improv troupe and continued to book stand-up gigs. All the while, Fallon remained fixated on joining *SNL*, his Holy Grail of comedy. As Fallon himself admits:

> This was my ultimate goal. If I ever cut into a birthday cake and made a wish, I would wish to be on *SNL*. If I threw a coin into a fountain, I would wish to be on *SNL*. If I saw a shooting star, I would wish to be on *SNL*. I remember saying to myself, "If I don't make it on [the show] before I'm 25, I'm going to kill myself." It's crazy. I had no other plan. I didn't have friends, I didn't have a girlfriend, I didn't have anything going on. I had my career, that was it.

Fallon unsuccessfully auditioned for the show in 1997 but continued to send videotapes of his stand-up set to *SNL* producers. He finally got a second shot at *SNL* at age twenty-three, doing killer impressions of Jerry Seinfeld, Chris Rock, Bill Cosby, and Adam Sandler—the latter even getting a laugh from the normally straight-faced Lorne Michaels.

Head writer Tina Fey was also on hand for Fallon's *SNL* audition and later noted: "He's one of two people I've ever seen who was completely ready to be on the show. Kristen Wiig is the other one . . . And Jimmy was ready—like, if there had been a show to do that night." Three weeks later, Fallon met with Lorne again in LA and was informed that he got the show. He was euphoric.

Much of Fallon's "swagger" came not from his confidence, but from his focus and dedication. His single-minded mission to land a gig on *SNL* paid off, and by the fourth episode of Fallon's first season of the show, he was already considered a breakout star.

Fallon enjoyed a very successful run on *SNL*, even becoming co-host of *Weekend Update* alongside Tina Fey. The *Update* slot gave Fallon additional exposure, which he used as a springboard to explore other projects, including writing a book called *I Hate This Place: The Pessimist's Guide to Life*. He also recorded a Grammy-nominated comedy album, *The Bathroom Wall*, and was host of the MTV Music Awards in 2001 and 2002.

Like dozens of *SNL* alumni before him, Fallon began transitioning to a movie career in 2004. His first film, *Taxi*, was met with tepid critical and audience reviews, and 2005's *Fever Pitch*, with Drew Barrymore, didn't fare much better. The movies were Fallon's first experience with failure, and he spent a couple of aimless years out of the limelight.

With the help and influence of Lorne Michaels, Fallon was named the new host of *Late Night*, succeeding Conan O'Brien in 2009. Initially, he was considered an odd choice for the job, by both skeptical NBC executives and the general public.

Late Night with Jimmy Fallon debuted in early 2009 to mixed reviews. It took some time for Fallon and the show to find its footing, but *Late Night* eventually caught on and found an audience with Fallon's heavier emphasis on music, impersonations, and games. *Late Night* was also the first show to tap into social media, with several sketches, such as Fallon and pal Justin Timberlake performing the "History of Rap," becoming a viral sensation on YouTube.

Fallon found his unique brand of comedy and distinguished *Late Night* as a serious comedy contender. It was Fallon's special style of humor that *New York* magazine called "the comedy of unabashed celebration." The 2010 *New York* article by Adam Sternbergh went on to say: "If other late-night shows have come to feature a familiar crankiness—directed at politicians, our trashy culture, or rival talk-show hosts—Fallon, by contrast, now presides over a goofy, raucous, playful, innovative hour of shameless shenanigans. It's Jimmy Fallon's late-night house of joy."

By 2013, Fallon was pulling down $11 million a year as host of *Late Night*, and speculation was already swirling about the possibility of Fallon taking over *The Tonight Show* from Jay Leno. NBC confirmed the rumors, and Jimmy Fallon became the sixth permanent host of *The Tonight Show* in February 2014. The show's debut was seen by 11.3 million viewers, the largest audience for a late-night show in recent memory.

Fallon has been called "Mr. Sunshine" and has been accused of laughing too much—breaking up in sketches, cracking up before and after jokes. Some have argued that Fallon cracks up to steal a scene or because he's unprofessional or smug. *New York* magazine's Sternbergh offered a much more likely scenario: "Maybe Fallon laughs so much because he's just having a really good time."

Since taking over *The Tonight Show*, Fallon has earned consistent ratings, routinely beating time-slot competitors Jimmy Kimmel and David Letterman (prior to his retirement). Reviews of the show's debut with Fallon were generally positive, with *The New York Times*'s Alessandra Stanley calling the show's premiere "more sweet than sassy," calling Fallon "the grateful heir, the eager freshman, the class clown with top grades and a good heart, someone older viewers can embrace without fear of being mocked or overlooked."

Meanwhile, *Entertainment Weekly* summarized the show's inaugural year: "In his first year as host of *The Tonight Show*, Fallon turned the revered late-night franchise into the hottest party in town, a celebrity playpen full of games, music, surprise guests, and good vibes all around."

Much of Fallon's success is a result of his creativity and innovation. From *SNL* to *Late Night*, and now on *The Tonight Show*, Fallon has taken risks, pushed the creative envelope, and stretched the limits of his medium of television. Such inventiveness is expected on *Saturday Night Live*, but many people assumed that Fallon would have to water down his creativeness to appeal to a broader audience for the more mainstream *Tonight Show*. On the contrary, Fallon has added more fun and originality to his version of the show, and it's paid off in ratings and viewers.

Fallon has also demonstrated his creativity with YouTube and social media. He has led the way when it comes to embracing social media, even "crowd sourcing" his jokes by getting viewers to submit jokes based on Twitter hashtags. Many of Fallon's sketches have gone "viral" on YouTube, proving Fallon's ability to expand beyond the traditional definition of television. For instance, his "Lip Sync Battle with Emma Stone" video has garnered 63 million views, six times the average audience for Fallon's *Tonight Show*.

His creativity and "think way outside the box" approach to entertainment and comedy have given us such unexpected gems as Madonna and Fallon's house band The Roots playing Madonna's "Holiday" with children's classroom musical instruments, news anchor Brian Williams in a mash-up of Snoop Dogg's "Gin and Juice," and even President Barack Obama doing a "slow jam" of the news. It's hard to imagine Johnny Carson or Jay Leno taking creative chances like that!

9

COMMUNICATION

"Wise men speak because they have something to say; fools because they have to say something."

—Plato

Paul J. Meyer, often credited as the father of the personal development industry, once said: "Communication—the human connection—is the key to personal and career success." The ability to communicate clearly and effectively affects virtually every aspect of our lives, and can mean the difference between failure and success in life.

Mastering communication skills can give you confidence, charisma, and clout! Consider Ronald Reagan—often called

"The Great Communicator"—who rose from humble roots in a small town in Illinois to become a broadcaster, actor, governor of California, and finally the fortieth president of the United States.

His ability to connect with Americans made him a popular president. He had a 68% approval rating when he left office, one of the highest approval ratings for presidents in the modern era. Reagan is often cited in various polls and surveys as one of the top ten presidents of all time.

His popularity and success as a president were due in large part to his communication skills and his folksy, plain-spoken style. The combination of his age—he was the oldest president—and his soft-spoken tone gave him a warm, grandfatherly image.

In an In-Depth Special feature titled "The Reagan Years: 'The Great Communicator' strikes chord with public," CNN summarized the Reagan presidency as follows:

> In a time when dazzling visual imagery was changing the face of communications, Ronald Reagan made use of the simple spoken word to define his political life. His language gave meaning to a national triumph, comforted Americans in a national tragedy and made complex international policy disputes understandable to millions. He spoke in clear, simple terms—too simple, his critics said—and painted vivid pictures that sometimes reflected a reality of his own making.
>
> Reagan put the speaking talent he honed as a Hollywood actor into the service of deeply rooted conservative

political beliefs: reduction of the size and scope of government, confrontation of the Soviet Union with massive military hardware and a clear moral distinction of ideologies, and the celebration of traditional American values.

His closest aides, as well as his biographers, support the notion that Reagan deserved his nickname of "The Great Communicator." Ronald Reagan's optimism and humor also helped endear him to the American people—which is yet another lesson we can take to use in our life and business. He was always upbeat and optimistic, and his uplifting "Morning in America" ad campaign helped him win reelection in 1984.

Here's that ad copy for those not old enough to remember it:

> It's morning again in America. Today more men and women will go to work than ever before in our country's history. With interest rates at about half the record highs of 1980, nearly 2,000 families today will buy new homes, more than at any time in the past four years. This afternoon 6,500 young men and women will be married, and with inflation at less than half of what it was just four years ago, they can look forward with confidence to the future. It's morning again in America, and under the leadership of President Reagan, our country is prouder and stronger and better. Why would we ever want to return to where we were less than four short years ago?

Reagan was known to joke frequently during his lifetime, and he displayed humor throughout his presidency. His numerous jokes and one-liners have been called classic quips—once again displaying the power of effective communication. He even made jokes about his own assassination attempt, telling the media he "forgot to duck." Then there was the classic microphone test before one of his weekly radio addresses when he joked, "My fellow Americans, I'm pleased to tell you today that I've signed legislation that will outlaw Russia forever. We begin bombing in five minutes." Ironically, instead of causing a scandal, the wisecrack seemed to endear him to the American public.

As the *BBC News* reported in 1989 at the end of his second term, Reagan told reporters:

> I won the nickname the great communicator, but I never thought it was my style that made a difference—it was the content.
>
> I wasn't a great communicator, but I communicated great things, and they didn't spring full blown from my brow, they came from the heart of a great nation, from our experience, our wisdom, and our belief in the principles that have guided us for two centuries.

If being a great communicator can help a poor farm boy become one of the most powerful and popular presidents of the twentieth century, imagine what it can do for me and you! The ability to communicate our ideas is the key to leadership.

Think of some of the most charismatic figures in history:

JFK, Martin Luther King Jr., Bill Clinton, Maya Angelou . . . All of them were great communicators. And while they were also skilled orators, communication skills go beyond public speaking. Once again, it's about building that connection with people! Establishing a real sense of connection will do wonders in improving your communications.

Eight Ways to Be a Better Communicator

1. **Listen more than you speak**—In our device-crazed, attention-deficit, glued-to-our-mobile-phone society, listening has become the new currency. These days, most people are constantly distracted and multitasking—and that makes really listening an even more valuable commodity. Listening shows respect, and giving the other person the gift of our full attention will go a long way in improving communication and connection.

2. **Ask questions**—Closely related to listening is asking questions of the other person. This shows your genuine interest in the other person and keeps the conversation on track. By asking thoughtful, clarifying questions, you reduce distractions and maintain your connection. As the saying goes, "It's more important to be interested than to be interesting."

3. **Build trust and empathy**—Communication is a two-way street, and showing empathy helps you see the other person's viewpoint. As you put yourself in their shoes, you're increasing your understanding and compassion.

This builds the "know, like, and trust" factor that is crucial for any relationship—whether it's at home or at work.

4. **Understand the value of face time**—With the advent of email, texting, and social media, communication has become much more impersonal and, in many ways, much more challenging. It's easy for emails or text messages to be misconstrued, so the value of face-to-face communication is even more impactful. We've all heard horror stories of people breaking up via text or getting fired via email. Avoid miscommunications and misunderstandings by meeting in person. At the very least, you can use videoconferencing to give you the face-to-face feel.

5. **Leave your ego at the door**—Egos, arrogance, and overbearing personalities have no place in good communications. Back when music producer Quincy Jones was bringing together the day's greatest rock stars to record "We Are the World," he knew he'd be dealing with a lot of strong personalities. To keep the A-list stars in line, Jones simply posted a "Check your ego at the door" sign. By keeping egos out of the project, the campaign was a huge success.

6. **Consider your body language**—What you do can be as important as what you say, so you've got to keep your body language in mind during your communications. Nonverbal cues can communicate much more than we

may think. Everything from eye contact to body posture sends a strong message, so we must remain aware of what we're saying even when we're not speaking! Remember that you're constantly communicating even if you're not saying a word.

7. **Tell stories**—Storytelling is one of the most powerful communications tools at our disposal, yet we often simply state facts rather than share stories. Research shows that stories actually activate our brains and make us more persuasive. Think about how you can use the power of stories to make your communications more memorable and effective. At the end of the day it's not what you say, it's how you make them feel.

8. **Close the loop**—It's also very important to end your communication by being clear about follow-up, expectations, or next steps. Avoid leaving any "open loops" in the communication. Be clear about what actions need to be taken and who is accountable. Being clear about what's next will avoid conflict and confusion. Closing the loop will clean up your communications!

Earlier we mentioned the power of storytelling and how it can greatly enhance your communication skills. Pixar storyboard artist Emma Coats compiled an amazing list of storytelling tips she collected over her years of working with the famed animation studio. Here are 22 Story Basics, sometimes known online as "Pixar's Twenty-Two Rules of Storytelling":

1. You admire a character for trying more than for their successes.
2. You gotta keep in mind what's interesting to you as an audience, not what's fun to do as a writer. They can be very different.
3. Trying for theme is important, but you won't see what the story is actually about 'til you're at the end of it. Now rewrite.
4. Once upon a time there was ___ . Every day, ___ . One day ___ . Because of that, ___ . Because of that, ___ . Until finally ___ . (Story Spine, from Kenn Adams)
5. Simplify. Focus. Combine characters. Hop over detours. You'll feel like you're losing valuable stuff but it sets you free.
6. What is your character good at, comfortable with? Throw the polar opposite at them. Challenge them. How do they deal?
7. Come up with your ending before you figure out your middle. Seriously! Endings are hard, get yours working up front.
8. Finish your story, let go even if it's not perfect. In an ideal world you have both, but move on. Do better next time.
9. When you're stuck, make a list of what WOULDN'T

happen next. Lots of times the material to get you unstuck will show up.

10. Pull apart the stories you like. What you like in them is a part of you; you've got to recognize it before you can use it.
11. Putting it on paper lets you start fixing it. If it stays in your head, a perfect idea, you'll never share it with anyone.
12. Discount the 1st thing that comes to mind. And the 2nd, 3rd, 4th, 5th—get the obvious out of the way. Surprise yourself.
13. Give your characters opinions. Passive/malleable might seem likable to you as you write, but it's poison to the audience.
14. Why must you tell THIS story? What's the belief burning within you that your story feeds off of? That's the heart of it.
15. If you were your character, in this situation, how would you feel? Honesty lends credibility to unbelievable situations.
16. What are the stakes? Give us reason to root for the character. What happens if they don't succeed? Stack the odds against.
17. No work is ever wasted. If it's not working, let go and move on—it'll come back around to be useful later.

18. You have to know yourself: the difference between doing your best & fussing. Story is testing, not refining.

19. Coincidences to get characters into trouble are great; coincidences to get them out of it are cheating.

20. Exercise: take the building blocks of a movie you dislike. How would you rearrange them into what you DO like?

21. You gotta identify with your situation/characters, can't just write 'cool'. What would make YOU act that way?

22. What's the essence of your story? Most economical telling of it? If you know that, you can build out from there.

SWAGGER SUCCESS STORY

JORDAN SPIETH

Swagger comes in all shapes, sizes, and ages. And if you're looking for proof that swagger doesn't need to be loud or flashy, look no further than twenty-two-year-old Jordan Spieth, currently (as of this writing) the number-one golfer in the world, according to the Official World Golf Rankings.

The Dallas native turned pro halfway through his sophomore year at the University of Texas and seemingly came out of nowhere to take the golf world by storm. Spieth won both the Masters Tournament and the U.S. Open in 2015, becoming only the sixth player ever to win the Masters and the U.S. Open back to back, and the first since Tiger Woods in 2002.

Spieth won his first major at the 2015 Masters Tournament, earning him a cool $1.8 million. He tied the seventy-two-hole record set by Tiger Woods in 1997 and became the second youngest to win the Masters, behind Woods. He then won the 2015 U.S. Open with a final score of 5 under par, making him the youngest U.S. Open champion since Bobby Jones in 1923.

All this success hasn't gone to the young golfer's head, with everyone agreeing that Spieth has remained humble and grounded. *The Salt Lake Tribune* noted that Jordan is "still the kid next door," and went on to comment, "Spieth is still the kid who throws you the paper and passes the communion plate. He is not linebacker-size, he is not an especially long driver, and when he takes off his cap, his hairline is even retreating. Such talent is not often wrapped in such a comfortable shell."

Jordan's parents, Shawn and Chris, joined the Brookhaven Country Club in Dallas when Jordan was eight years old, because they liked the club's family atmosphere. His father, Shawn, played baseball at Lehigh, while his mom, Chris, was a Division III basketball player. Jordan's six-foot-six brother Steven plays basketball at Brown University. His younger sister, Ellie, thirteen, is Jordan's hero and inspiration. As *Golfweek* shares, "Ellie's special needs have taught the family more about patience and perseverance than any test of golf."

Spieth first showed an interest in golf while at summer camp, when he noticed some older boys hitting golf balls at the driving range. He told his mother he wanted to try it, and, as *Golfweek* noted, "Before she knew it, a self-taught Spieth was winning golf tournaments."

As Beth Ann Nichols of *Golfweek* wrote, "At age 11, Spieth easily won his age division at the Starburst Junior Golf Classic in Waco, Texas. The next year he told his parents he wanted to play in the championship division, which included kids up to 18 years old. 'You're 12,' they reminded him. Jordan didn't care. He didn't want to win a trophy for beating kids his age. He wanted a trophy for beating everyone. The summer after seventh grade, Spieth won the championship division."

"My dad told me growing up, 'You've got to start setting goals,'" says Spieth. "That's been my philosophy, set goals and work hard, stay focused, and reach them as soon as possible. At each level, I always reevaluate my goals and establish new ones. I never want to become complacent, but always push myself further."

Spieth's focus has served him well. In both 2009 and 2011, Spieth won the U.S. Junior Amateur, joining Tiger Woods as its only multiple winners. Spieth accepted an exemption to play in the PGA Tour's HP Byron Nelson Championship in 2010. It was the event's first amateur exemption since 1995. Jordan made the cut, becoming the sixth-youngest player to make the cut at a PGA Tour event.

In 2011, Spieth graduated from the Jesuit College Preparatory School of Dallas and entered his beloved University of Texas, where he played college golf for the Longhorns. In his freshman year at Texas, Spieth won three events and led the team in scoring average. He also helped his team win the NCAA championship, was named to the All-Big 12 Team, was named Big 12 Freshman of the Year and Player of the Year, and was a first-team All-American. Spieth is a self-professed die-hard Texas sports fan and, while at UT, he spent as much time at football, basketball, and baseball games as possible. "I'm as big a Longhorn fan as you'll find," admits Spieth.

Halfway through his sophomore year at UT, nineteen-year-old Spieth made the decision to leave college and turn pro. "The hardest part of the decision was telling my teammates that I won't be competing with them," Spieth admitted. "Coach Fields and the players have all been real supportive. It's bittersweet, but they understand. This is my lifelong dream."

As *The Dallas Morning News* reported at the time, "For all intents and purposes, he was a college dropout searching for steady work, a gifted young actor with unlimited potential and no stage. But Spieth nailed the audition, and after one of the best rookie seasons ever, he is living the dream."

"I just remember that drive home was the worst," Spieth told *The Dallas Morning News*. "I wasn't going to change my mind about turning pro, but all that stuff was in my head." At the time, he was still driving the same beat-up car he had in high school, with over 100,000 miles on it. A few months later, Spieth boarded a private jet to Scotland to play in the British Open.

By September 2013, Spieth was named PGA Tour Rookie of the Year, and by the end of the year he was ranked tenth on the PGA Tour money list and twenty-second in the Official World Golf Rankings. Not bad for a twenty-year-old kid next door . . .

Spieth's amazing ascent continued into 2014, where his performance at the Masters put him into the top-ten world rankings for the first time. By March 2015, his victories at the Valspar Championship and the Valero Texas Open moved him to a career-high ranking of fourth in the world.

In 2015, having won the Masters in April and the U.S. Open in June and tying for fourth in July's British Open, Spieth was attempting to join Tiger Woods (2000) and Ben Hogan (1953) as the only male golfers to win three professional majors in a calendar year.

While Spieth lost the PGA Championship by just three shots, his poise under pressure all year and graciousness in defeat made it difficult to fathom that this was only his third full PGA Tour season. Despite the loss, and just seventy-one tournaments into his pro career, he became the world's number-one-ranked golfer.

The tournament's winner, Jason Day, had nothing but praise for the young golfer. "To be honest, the kid just doesn't go away," Day said of Spieth in *The Dallas Morning News*. "It just baffles me, the stuff he can prove out there. Obviously with the level of play that he's been playing this year, it's no wonder he's No. 1 in the world right now."

"It's all run together. It all happened quickly, sometimes it feels like a long time ago," admits Spieth. "And sometimes it feels like yesterday. All in all, it's really cool." Cool, calm, and collected seems to be Spieth's M.O. And all that poise and humility despite his meteoric rise gives Spieth swagger to spare.

10

CARING

"Never believe that a few caring
people can't change the world.
For, indeed, that's all who ever have."

—Margaret Mead

The idea of "caring" in business may sound a bit too "warm and fuzzy" or "touchy-feely" for some leaders. Perhaps they don't want to be seen as too soft or vacillating. Of course you don't want to be a pushover, but being a caring boss or manager does not mean coddling or babying your employees—and it doesn't mean being spineless. It's simply a matter of genuinely giving a damn about your employees and doing what's right for everyone, not just yourself.

Caring means showing compassion and character so your employees will admire and look up to you. In fact, a *Harvard Business Review* study found that "CEOs whose employees gave them high marks for character had an average return on assets of 9.35% over a two-year period. That's nearly five times as much as what those with low character ratings had; their return on assets averaged only 1.93%."

Caring also means holding yourself to the same standards as your company's employees. Staffers may resent a CEO who has a different set of rules than employees. To maintain the respect of your employees, you can't afford to be out of touch or too far removed from the day to day.

In the earlier chapters on "community" and "communications," we talked about the importance of MBWA, or "management by walking around." That same "in the trenches" mentality is equally important for showing you care about your employees.

Author and businessman Arnold H. Glasow said, "A good leader takes a little more than his share of the blame, and a little less than his share of the credit." And President Harry Truman echoed, "It is amazing what you can accomplish if you do not care who gets the credit." I've always been a big proponent of the "share the credit, take the blame" philosophy. You can build great loyalty once your employees know that you'll never "throw them under the bus." Take care of your employees and they will take care of you!

Netflix made the news when it announced its "unlimited" vacation policy and paternity/maternity leave. Richard Branson and Virgin followed their example, offering as many vacation days as employees want, so long as "their absence will not in any way damage the business—or, for that matter, their careers!"

Similarly, Netflix doesn't saddle their employees with draconian rules and regulations. Their expense policy, for example, is just five words long: "Act in Netflix's best interest." These flexible policies treat employees like adults who don't have to be babysat or constantly monitored. This also builds a culture of trust, caring, and compassion.

Facebook COO Sheryl Sandberg, who was the chief talent officer for Netflix when they put many of their generous policies in place, explains the Netflix philosophy: "Over the years we learned that if we asked people to rely on logic and common sense instead of on formal policies, most of the time we would get better results, and at lower cost. If you're careful to hire people who will put the company's interests first, who understand and support the desire for a high-performance workplace, 97% of your employees will do the right thing. Most companies spend endless time and money writing and enforcing HR policies to deal with problems the other 3% might cause. Instead, we tried really hard to not hire those people, and we let them go if it turned out we'd made a hiring mistake."

Sandberg says that the Netflix compensation policy followed the same basic philosophy: Be honest and treat people like adults. "For instance," says Sandberg, "during my tenure, Netflix didn't pay performance bonuses, because we believed that they're unnecessary if you hire the right people. If your employees are fully formed adults who put the company first, an annual bonus won't make them work harder or smarter. We also believed in market-based pay and would tell employees that it was smart to interview with competitors when they had the chance, in order to get a good sense of the market rate for their talent. Many HR people dislike it when employees talk to recruiters, but I always told employees to take the call, ask how much, and send me the number—it's valuable information."

This contrarian approach to salaries and compensation demonstrated that Netflix cared about their employees, and the philosophy has paid off for Netflix. "People find the Netflix approach to talent and culture compelling for a few reasons," says Sandberg. "The most obvious one is that Netflix has been really successful: During 2013 alone its stock more than tripled, it won three Emmy awards, and its U.S. subscriber base grew to nearly 29 million. All that aside, the approach is compelling because it derives from common sense."

Turns out that caring and common sense go hand in hand. So, weaving "caring" into your company culture may not be as complicated as we often make it. Simply do the right thing!

Seven Ways to Create a Culture of Caring

1. **Really Listen to Your Employees**—It's one thing to have an "open door policy," but truly listening to your employees has to be more than just lip service. Take time to sit down with your coworkers—individually and collectively—and give them the opportunity to have a voice. Personal development author Bryant H. McGill

reminds us "One of the most sincere forms of respect is actually listening to what another has to say."

2. **Create Bonding Opportunities**—Employees who play together, stay together! Make sure your employees have the chance to really get to know one another, both inside and outside the workplace. Whether you have events and activities at the office, or take company field trips or retreats, be sure to provide opportunities for your team to have fun together.

3. **Provide Opportunities to Give Back to the Community**—One of the best ways you can develop bonding opportunities is to allow your employees time off to volunteer and give back to the community. Many companies like ours offer paid time off for community service. Some larger corporations, such as Deloitte, offer "unlimited" time off for volunteering. Deloitte also does an annual "Impact Day," where 28,000 employees from eighty offices participate in their yearly day of service.

4. **Offer Unique Benefits and Perks**—To remain competitive and attract the best workers, company benefits these days have to go beyond the standard two or three weeks of vacation. That's why more employers are getting creative with their perks. If you can offer something no one else can, you'll have an extra advantage. Being in the ticket business, TicketCity gives our team members opportunities to attend "once-in-a-lifetime" events like the Olympics. Other companies, like

Google, are known for their generous perks, such as oil changes and car washes, massages and yoga, backup child-care assistance, and up to $12,000 annually in tuition reimbursement.

5. **Lead by Example**—Obviously, it takes more than ping-pong tables and yoga classes to create a culture of caring. For caring to become a core value of your company, it has to start at the top. If you're going to create an atmosphere conducive to caring, the CEO has to take the lead and set the example. Managers and staff will ultimately take their cue from the boss. Former IBM Chairman Thomas Watson once said: "Nothing so conclusively proves a man's ability to lead others, as what he does from day to day to lead himself."

6. **Be Available to Your Employees**—If you want your staff to be dedicated and responsive, then you've got to be responsive to them. Make yourself available and accessible to your employees, and give them opportunities for personal, one-on-one time with you. Needless to say, this gets more challenging with a bigger company, but workers appreciate knowing their voice can be heard, and in this day of "always connected" technology, there's no reason not to connect with your remote employees through Skype, FaceTime, Google Hangouts, or other videoconferencing technology.

7. **Empower Your People**—An often-overlooked aspect of creating a caring culture is to give your employees

> the power to make decisions without being micromanaged. Simon Sinek, author of *Start with Why: How Great Leaders Inspire Everyone to Take Action*, and TED Talk speaker says on his blog, *Re:Focus, Simple Ideas to Help You Thrive*, that empowered employees provide exceptional service. "Empowered employees have the power to make decisions without a supervisor. They are entitled to go off script, bend the rules, and do what they see fit if they believe it is the right thing to do for the customer. More than any other kind of employee, the empowered employee is able to create a feeling of true customer service that ultimately yields much greater customer loyalty." Creating a caring culture is not only good for employees, it's also good for business. *The Harvard Business Review* reports on a study that says: "Employees who felt they worked in a loving, caring culture reported higher levels of satisfaction and teamwork."

The Harvard Business Review goes on to point out that "Some large, well-known organizations are already leading the pack in creating cultures of companionate love. Whole Foods Market has a set of management principles that begin with 'Love,' and PepsiCo lists 'caring' as its first guiding principle on its website. Zappos also explicitly focuses on caring as part of its values: 'We are more than a team though . . . we are a family. We watch out for each other, care for each other and go above and beyond for each other.'"

Of course, it's not enough to be a leader who cares about your people—you've also got to care about your customers! The good news is that caring for your employees typically translates to those employees caring for your customers. It's a relatively simple formula: Take good care of your employees and they'll take good care of your customers.

Brands like Zappos, Amazon, Google, Southwest Airlines, and Marriott are known for their exceptional customer service. Many of these leading companies prefer to think of it not in terms of their customer "service," but the customer "experience."

Denise Lee Yohn, author of *What Great Brands Do: The Seven Brand-Building Principles That Separate the Best from the Rest*, says that it's the emotional connections that lead to true brand loyalty and customer satisfaction.

In her *Forbes* magazine feature on brand-building, Denise Lee Yohn used Virgin America as an example of a company that builds long-lasting, emotional connections with its customers.

We strive to do the same here at TicketCity. We do more than just sell tickets. We consider ourselves to be in the business of providing unforgettable experiences and making memories that will last a lifetime. Because we provide access to any ticket for any event around the world, we really are giving our customers once-in-a-lifetime experiences. Today we have over 225,000 loyal clients in more than seventy countries. We love meeting our clients face-to-face at concerts and sporting events, and we take great pride in going above and beyond to enhance their experience.

That's why we love getting feedback from our customers like this:

"Wow! What a weekend in East Lansing. Thanks to TicketCity I was able to celebrate my son's 13th birthday with family and friends on a beautiful fall day! Thanks again, TicketCity, for making me a hero in my son's eyes!"

"My son and I have season tickets to the Thunder, I wanted to surprise him with seats lower than we have. It was great to see the players close up. Thank You, TicketCity, for making that happen."

ESPN's Chris Fowler is also a big fan—so much so that we made him our Brand Ambassador! Here's what Chris has to say about us:

"TicketCity is my go-to place for sports tickets. With TicketCity's 24/7 expert service, free shipping and on-site event staff, I know I'm going to have a great experience all the way to game time. I can always count on an excellent selection of sports tickets, and their easy to use website means finding the tickets I need is easy. Plus, I like knowing that when I purchase tickets from TicketCity, I'm working with folks who love these events as much as I do."

At the end of the day, we're just fans helping fans find tickets. And because we have a passion for what we do, it makes building that emotional connection with our customers much more meaningful. Of course, we realize that customer satisfaction is an ongoing, daily journey and not a destination—but we strive to do our best every day. Love what you do, do it well, and keep on doing it. That's the way to instill caring in your company!"

SWAGGER SUCCESS STORY

OPRAH WINFREY

You may not think "swagger" when you hear the name Oprah—at least not in the traditional sense of the word. Oprah may not personify the same type of swagger as a Mick Jagger, Frank Sinatra, or JFK, but you can't deny her incredible power, her worldwide influence, and her astronomical level of success.

One of only a handful of people in the world known by her first name, the "Queen of All Media" has been ranked the richest African-American of the twentieth century and the greatest black philanthropist in American history. She is currently America's only black billionaire, with an estimated net worth of $3 billion. Numerous polls and media identify her as the most influential woman in the world, and CNN has called her "the world's most powerful woman."

"Self-made" doesn't begin to describe Oprah's amazing ascent—her swagger, confidence, and charisma were forged over the years and developed out of a background of poverty, abuse, and hardship. She was born dirt poor in Kosciusko, Mississippi, to an unwed teenage mother, who moved north shortly after her birth. As a result, Oprah was raised for her first six years by her grandmother, Hattie Mae Lee, who taught her to read and recite Bible verses. It was said she was so poor that she had to wear dresses made of potato sacks, and she was ridiculed by her classmates at school. She found some solace at the local church, where Oprah earned the nickname "The Preacher" for her ability to remember and recite Bible verses.

At age six, she moved north to an inner-city neighborhood in Milwaukee to join her mother, Vernita Lee, who was working as a maid. When Lee could no longer support her daughter, she was sent to live with her father, Vernon Winfrey, in Nashville, Tennessee.

Oprah later admitted that she was repeatedly molested and abused during childhood. She was raped at age nine and became pregnant at fourteen, but her son died in infancy. After years of abuse and bouncing back and forth from her mother to father, Oprah ran away from home at age thirteen. Eventually, she returned to live with her father, who was strict but supportive. He made education a priority for the teenager, and she became an honor student and skilled orator.

Oprah joined the speech team at East Nashville High School and placed second in the nation in dramatic interpretation. She also won an oratory contest, which earned her a full scholarship to Tennessee State University, where she studied Communications. At seventeen, Oprah won the Miss Black Tennessee beauty pageant and gained the attention of the local black radio station, who hired her part-time to do the news.

She continued to work in the local media and became both the youngest news anchor and the first black female news anchor at Nashville's WLAC-TV. She credits her grandmother, Hattie Mae, for encouraging her to speak in public, and for giving her a positive self-image, despite her difficult childhood.

After working on-air in Nashville, Winfrey moved to Baltimore in 1976 to co-anchor the six o'clock news on WJZ-TV. She later became the co-host for WJZ-TV's local talk show, *People Are Talking.* In 1983, Oprah moved to Chicago, a much larger TV market, for an opportunity to host WLS-TV's morning talk show, *AM Chicago.* With Oprah as host, the low-rated talk show went from worst to first and overtook *Donahue* as the highest-rated talk show in Chicago.

While Oprah began to find success on a national level, she never used her difficult upbringing as a crutch. As she put it: "I don't think of myself as a poor deprived ghetto girl who made good. I think of myself as somebody who from an early age knew I was responsible for myself, and I had to make good."

Movie critic and friend Roger Ebert encouraged Oprah to bring her show into national syndication, and she soon signed a syndication deal with King World. The new *Oprah Winfrey Show* began broadcasting nationally on September 8, 1986. It was an immediate hit, becoming the number-one daytime talk show—doubling then talk-show king Phil Donahue's national audience.

At the time, much was made of Oprah's dethroning Phil Donahue as the top talk-show host. In an August 8, 1988 *Time* magazine feature titled "Oprah Winfrey: Lady with a Calling," Richard Zoglin wrote:

> Few people would have bet on Oprah Winfrey's swift rise to host of the most popular talk show on TV. In a field dominated by white males, she is a black female of ample bulk. As interviewers go, she is no match for, say, Phil Donahue. What she lacks in journalistic toughness, she makes up for in plainspoken

> curiosity, robust humor and, above all, empathy. Guests with sad stories to tell are apt to rouse a tear in Oprah's eye. They, in turn, often find themselves revealing things they would not imagine telling anyone, much less a national TV audience. It is the talk show as a group therapy session.

Meanwhile, *LA Times* TV critic Howard Rosenberg called Oprah "a roundhouse, a full course meal, big, brassy, loud, aggressive, hyper, laughable, lovable, soulful, tender, low-down, earthy and hungry. And she may know the way to Phil Donahue's jugular." *Newsday* noted: "Oprah Winfrey is sharper than Donahue, wittier, more genuine, and far better attuned to her audience, if not the world." Oprah was well on her way to making television history.

Oprah has been credited with creating a more intimate and "confessional" brand of talk show, but she is also thought to have popularized and revolutionized the tabloid-talk-show genre. Her early career may have been considered "tabloid" TV, but by the mid-1990s she had reinvented her show with a focus on literature, self-improvement, spirituality, and celebrity interviews. She also became famous for hosting televised giveaways where every audience member would receive a new car or an exotic vacation.

As Oprah's show continued to grow in popularity, she expanded her activities and grew her media empire. She created Harpo Productions (Oprah spelled backward) as a media production company for her many ventures, and began starring in television specials and films—most notably *The Color Purple*, for which she was nominated for an Oscar for Best Supporting Actress. Her 1993 celebrity interview with Michael Jackson became the most-watched television interview of all time, with an audience of over 36 million viewers.

In addition to hosting and appearing on television, Oprah co-founded the women's cable television network Oxygen in 2000. The network reaches over 77 million Americans and was sold to NBC Universal in 2007 for $925 million. In 2011, Oprah partnered with Discovery Communications to launch OWN: Oprah Winfrey Network. The new channel reaches nearly 82 million homes.

Once her long-running and enormously popular *Oprah Winfrey Show* aired its final broadcast in May 2011, Oprah was able to devote more of her time to the new OWN cable network. As Oprah told the *Hollywood Reporter*, "For all of those years on the *Oprah Show*, we were able to encapsulate the stories that connected to our audience in a way that nobody else could. I love telling the real stories of people's lives, and now we get to create them, make them up, and I get to be part of them as an actor and producer."

Besides her many television and film ventures, Oprah has co-authored five books and publishes *O, The Oprah Magazine*, with partner Hearst. *Fortune* called *O, The Oprah Magazine,* the most successful start-up ever in the publishing industry. Winfrey also created Oprah.com, which boasts over six million users per month. Her media empire also includes radio, and in 2006, she signed a $55-million-dollar deal to start Oprah Radio on the XM Satellite Radio network.

With Oprah's massive media footprint, and as many as 13 million viewers watching *The Oprah Winfrey Show* at its peak, Oprah's enormous influence became known as "The Oprah Effect." Her opinions and endorsements could turn books into instant best sellers. It was said that being featured on "Oprah's Book Club" could mean a million additional sales for an author.

Her authority expands well beyond books, as Oprah helped launch the careers of other talk-show "spin-offs" such as Dr. Phil, Dr. Oz, and

Rachael Ray. And her endorsement of presidential candidate Barack Obama in 2008 helped boost his campaign and get him elected. In fact, Oprah was then hailed as "the most instrumental person in electing Barack Obama president."

Oprah also sets the example and personifies caring as one of the most generous and philanthropic public figures alive. She was the first African-American to rank among the fifty most generous Americans, and has donated $400 million to educational causes.

Oprah also founded Oprah's Angel Network, a charity that supported charitable projects and provided grants to nonprofit organizations around the world. Oprah's Angel Network raised more than $80 million for charity.

Oprah Winfrey has taken the concept of caring to a whole new level, and her tireless philanthropic efforts raise the bar for other celebrities and businesses.

OWN IT!

We've looked at ten qualities of swaggerlicious success and given you some insights on ten people who have personified swagger. When all is said and done, swagger, confidence, power, coolness—whatever you want to call that killer self-assurance—really comes down to owning it. Own your value. Believe in yourself. Seize each day. Make your life matter!

Owning it is not a matter of being extroverted, loud, or boisterous. It doesn't matter if you're a man or a woman, bold or shy, young or old. It's simply about being comfortable in your own skin and being fully self-expressed. It's about being proud to be you! Once you've got a positive self-image and you "own it," you're on your way to having a happier, more fulfilled life.

Feel free to go back through any of the chapters anytime and review the ten Cs of success: collaboration, charisma, commitment, courage, coolness, competitiveness, character, creativity, communication, and caring. Refer back to our

Swagger Success Stories at the end of each chapter and see who can inspire and empower you.

Remember, Sir Richard Branson wasn't born with swagger. He was a failing student with dyslexia. His ambition, curiosity, and thirst for adventure made him a billionaire and cultural icon. Branson owns it with humor, charm, and flair.

Ronda Rousey's father took his own life when Ronda was just eight years old, and she has had some significant lows on her journey, including a period where she was drinking heavily and sleeping in her car. Still, her commitment, dedication, and resolve helped her persevere and become a champion. Ronda Rousey owns it and has defined what it means to be a great athlete.

Oprah's difficult childhood has been well documented, but she never used her upbringing as an excuse on the way to becoming the country's only black billionaire. Oprah owns it like no one else in the world.

Take a page from their playbooks and refuse to play small. Stand in your power. Appreciate your uniqueness. Resolve to be great and live large. When fear and self-doubt creep in, remember the wise words of best-selling author Marianne Williamson, who said: "Our deepest fear is not that we are inadequate. Our deepest fear is that we are powerful beyond measure. It is our light, not our darkness, that most frightens us. We ask ourselves, 'Who am I to be brilliant, gorgeous, talented, fabulous?' Actually, who are you not to be?"

Here's to "owning it" every day!

—Randy Cohen

WOO-WOO!!
CELEBRATING 27 YEARS IN BUSINESS WITH TICKETCITY

Ten Things I have Learned while Growing TicketCity

1. **Celebrate your victories.** Victory loves preparation, so prepare yourself to be victorious, then celebrate those wins.

2. **Treat your team like family.** Love your team. We work together and see them more often than our biological families. So be kind to them, trust them, and listen to them.

3. **Empower your team.** Empower your team to make decisions. The more they make, the better they will become at making them. My management team has been with me for an average of eighteen years each. Now you know why.

4. **Take risks.** Have the courage of your convictions. Be intentional and committed. You need to be able to trust yourself. Never overlook your intuition, and stop

second-guessing yourself. You have to be able to step up and stand firm. You think Martin Luther King Jr., Gandhi, and even Rosa Parks second-guessed themselves during their acts of bravery and defiance? No, they were authentic and intentional.

5. **Have fun.** Laugh, celebrate, high-five, play games, drink, eat, and live large. The journey should be full of smiles.

6. **Work hard and play hard.** Make bold declarations and deliver on them. Fortune favors the bold, so set daring, audacious objectives and make them happen. You will become more confident and courageous. Then have blowouts with your team celebrating your successes.

7. **Fight for what you believe in.** Plan your work and work your plan. Do the right thing long after the feeling of doing it leaves you. Never stop being passionate.

8. **Challenge one another to do more than what's expected.** Go above and beyond the call of duty. If others see you doing it, they will follow and go above and beyond themselves.

9. **Make money. Profit is important.** You're in business to make a difference, create wealth, and enhance the lives of others around you. In order to do this, you MUST be profitable. Pay attention and don't be afraid to say no to difficult questions that will result in losses. Think big picture. If a short-term loss will help a long-term gain, then go for it. If not, don't!

10. **Listen and treat clients with gratitude.** You have to master not only the art of listening to your head; you must also master listening to your heart and your gut. Then your authenticity will shine with gratitude and clients will feel appreciated and respected.

ACKNOWLEDGMENTS

I would like to thank Lou Bortone for all his hard work and research on *Secrets of Swagger.*

I would also like to thank my ACE (Austin Council of Entrepreneurs) group, my GOT (Gathering of Titans) group, my family, and all the TicketCitians out there who have helped make this life journey possible.

And finally, I would like to thank my dad Joel Cohen, who passed away this year, for all his love and guidance. I love you, Dad.

Thank you, thank you, thank you!!!

AUTHOR Q & A

Q: Do you have a special routine or practice you follow when you're writing? Do you have a special place where you write, and if so, would you describe it and why it's important to you?

A: I usually write in my office or journal in bed.

Q: Did anything occur during the course of writing this book that gave you a different perspective on the writing process and what it takes to be an author?

A: I realized how you do anything is how you do everything and the more you put into a project, the better it turns out.

Q: Would you tell us about a particular person or author who has had a fundamental influence on your writing or your philosophy of life and why that is?

A: I love marketers and business coaches like Seth Godin and Verne Harnish. They really care and want to make a difference in the lives of others.

Q: Was there a particular event in your life that made you first realize how important swagger is to success? Could you describe it and why it was significant?

A: When I was ten, our soccer coach said whoever practiced the hardest that week would get to go to a Washington Redskins game with him. I learned incentivication and the fact that I had better stand out if I wanted to win the opportunity. I worked hard and was able to attend my first Redskins game!

Q: Can you say a bit about how you came up with the various pieces of swagger you outline in the book? Would you share any personal experiences from your life that contributed to your unique take on swagger?

A: Diving into life and all its opportunities enabled me to find my style of swagger. I knew in order for me to achieve and succeed, I would have to put myself out there and find a way to show up and make it happen if I really wanted it bad enough. There is always a way and showing up is the first step.

Q: Which swagger factor is your favorite and why?

A: Courage. If you put yourself out there and are not afraid to take chances, anyone can achieve their dreams.

Q: It's clear that your knowledge of the struggles of celebrity is extensive. How did you come to know so much about fame?

A: Growing up in Austin, Texas, for the past thirty-three years—from high school to college to growing TicketCity—put me in the spotlight. Amazing opportunities have been created and I have been able to engage and learn from successful individuals and celebrities. Having access to tickets for prestige events around the world didn't hurt either.

Q: Do you have any amusing tidbits about any of the celebrities that didn't make it into the book that you might like to share?

A: Tony Hsieh, the CEO from Zappos, is so amazing in the way he engages in social media and turns an introverted personality into an extroverted lifestyle.

Q: Could you discuss who was your favorite of the iconic figures in the book to write about and why?

A: Richard Branson is my favorite because of his carefree, love-life personality. He is kind, generous, sweet, and an amazing listener.

Q: Could you describe whether writing one specific chapter or celebrity story was especially challenging (or especially fun) and why?

A: The chapter on coolness was tough because everyone has a different opinion on what it really means to be cool. Think about the movies *West Side Story* and *Warriors* if you have seen them. Different people were in different gangs because those clubs fit their personalities. That's why we tend to associate ourselves with individuals who are like-minded.

Q: Can you tell us what you think you might have done in life if you hadn't followed the path you did? Can you describe a turning point in your life that led you where you are today?

A: I would have been in sales or marketing at a Fortune 100 business, and after learning on their dime, I would have created my own entrepreneurial company.

Q: This is your second book. Did you always know that you wanted to follow *Ticket to the Limit* up with a book like this, or did something specific inspire you to write this book? Can you say a little bit about what inspired you to begin outlining your go-getter philosophy?

A: No, I never planned on writing another book. But when I thought of the opportunity to share some of my expertise and give back, and the fact that I could possibly help some people make a difference in their life and the lives of others, it was a no-brainer.

Q: Besides the knowledge of how to own their personal sense of swagger, what do you hope your readers will take away from this book? Do you have any final words for your readers?

A: (1) You grow fresh leadership within your organization. When you create leaders, they do remarkable things. They question the obvious and rationalize the outrageous. Leaders must be intentional. They figure out what the right thing to do is. It all starts with culture and an intentional culture is a strategic advantage and must be evangelized. Rational people acting in intentional ways always do the right thing. Who do *you* surround yourself with who has swagger and pushes you to improve daily through their success and encouragement? Make sure you seek out the people who spark growth in you.

(2) One of my favorite things to do is let seventh graders come into TicketCity once a year and become CEO for the day. They learn so much and I get so excited. I think it makes more of a difference in our employees' lives than it does in theirs! These kids learn the business and then have to actually make a difference in the company with what they've learned.

(3) Be true to yourself, follow your heart, be open, but most importantly—be authentic.

Q: Can we look forward to a third book sometime soon?

A: I never know what lies ahead, but as long as I keep paying attention it will be a super-fun journey with many lessons to share.

ABOUT THE AUTHOR

Randy Cohen is an entrepreneur, CEO, author, and philanthropist based out of Austin, Texas. Randy founded TicketCity in 1990, while he was a student at the University of Texas, with a few basketball tickets and $1,200. Since then, the company has grown into one of the largest privately held ticket marketplaces in the world, and Randy is considered among the most well-known and respected leaders in the ticket industry. In 2009, while serving as the CEO of TicketCity, Randy authored his first book, *Ticket to the Limit*, which depicts his personal account of how passion, purpose, and performance can transform life and business. Much of Randy's success can be attributed to his tireless enthusiasm and inescapable passion for excellence. Randy still loves finding the perfect seats for clients and empowering people to discover and utilize their passions.

In addition to serving as TicketCity's CEO, Randy is extremely active in the Austin community as a member of the Austin Council of Entrepreneurs, and has served on the board of directors of numerous other organizations. Randy graduated from the University of Texas as well as the Birthing of Giants program at MIT. He is the proud father of three and brother of two.